LEARN BLUES/ROCK
SOLOING
WITH THE MASTERS

BY TOBY WINE

Recording credits:
DOUG BODUCH, guitar
WARREN WIEGRATZ, keyboard
TOM MCGIRR, bass
SCOTT SCHROEDL, drums

Cherry Lane Music Company
Director of Publications: Mark Phillips

ISBN 978-1-60378-265-4

Visit Visit our website at
www.cherrylaneprint.com

CONTENTS

INTRODUCTION

Every day, legions of guitarists across the globe pick up their instruments and try their hand at the time-honored art of improvising a 12-bar blues solo. Taking into consideration the superstars and absolute beginners, studio aces and long time hobbyists, journeymen pros and teenaged acolytes, their number must surely run into the five figures, conservatively. But gather the players who are truly doing it well—with authenticity, soul, originality, passion, and finesse—and the number shrinks dramatically. In the pages that follow, we'll examine the work of six bona fide masters of the idiom. We'll learn licks, tricks, and techniques, working our way all the while towards the ultimate goal of building stronger solos regardless of our current skill level. With examples from a dozen classic recordings, this is blues soloing straight from the horse's mouth. Let's dig in and take our playing to the next level.

ABOUT THE AUTHOR

Toby Wine is a native New Yorker and a freelance guitarist, composer, arranger, and educator. He is a graduate of the Manhattan School of Music, where he studied composition with Manny Albam and Edward Green. Toby has performed with Philip Harper (of the Harper Brothers and Art Blakey's Jazz Messengers), Bob Mover, Ari Ambrose, Michael and Carolyn Leonhart (of Steely Dan), Peter Hartmann, Ian Hendrickson-Smith (of Sharon Jones and the Dap-Kings), Melee, Saycon (Fela!), Nakia Henry, and the Harlem-based rock band Kojomodibo Sun, among others. His arrangements and compositions can be heard on recordings by Tobias Gebb and Unit Seven (*Free at Last*, *Yummyhouse*), Phillip Harper (*Soulful Sin*, *The Thirteenth Moon*, Muse Records), Ari Ambrose (*Early Song*, Steeplechase), and Ian Hendrickson-Smith (*Up in Smoke*, Sharp Nine). Toby leads his own trio and septet, does studio sessions, and works as a sideman with a variety of tri-state area bandleaders. He spent four years as the music librarian for the Carnegie Hall Jazz band and is currently an instructor at the Church Street School for Music and Art in Tribeca. He is the author of numerous Cherry Lane publications, including *The Art of Texas Blues*, *150 Cool Jazz Licks in Tab*, *Johnny Winter Plays the Blues*, *Steely Dan: Legendary Licks*, and *Derek Trucks: Legendary Licks*.

ACKNOWLEDGMENTS

Many thanks are due to Cherry Lane's fearless leaders, John Stix and Mark Phillips. Thanks as well to my parents, Rosemary and Jerry, to my loving wife Christina, and to Bibi, Bob, Jack, Noah, Enid, Mover, Humph (R.I.P.), fellow author Karl Kaminski, and all the great teachers—and students—I've had. I've learned so much from all of you. And special thanks to Reggie and Pepper for sitting on all the music every time I tried to get any work done.

CHAPTER 1

The Artists and Their Songs

Joe Bonamassa (b.1977)

This young native of Utica, New York, has quickly established himself as a force to be reckoned with in both the blues and rock guitar worlds. Bonamassa is not only a formidably accomplished player of exceptional technical prowess, but also a font of knowledge in a wide variety of styles—from traditional blues to overdrive-soaked British blues rock, to country chicken pickin,' jazz, soul, and beyond. He both opened for B.B. King and found himself the protégé of the late, great Danny Gatton before he hit his teens but is no mere child prodigy resting on the laurels of his early success. He is a tireless worker and an inquisitive musician of the first order, constantly growing, maturing, and creating a body of work that is startling in its diversity and quality. For this book, we choose two songs from his 2003 release, *Blues Deluxe*. The title track is a slow and absolutely smoking rendition of an old gem by a somewhat unlikely songwriter (Rod Stewart), and the other is an uptempo, swinging cover of "Leftovers" by the late Texas blues master Albert Collins. Both songs are in the key of C and, while highly traditional, have Bonamassa's unmistakably original mark firmly attached.

Eric Clapton (b.1945)

"Old Slowhand" is one of the world's most influential and emulated guitarists and truly needs no introduction. His career, spanning work with Cream, the Yardbirds, John Mayall's Bluesbreakers, Derek & the Dominos, and more, in addition to extensive solo work and guest appearances, crosses stylistic boundaries and sets standards for taste, elegance, tone, and emotional intensity. His overdriven, unabashed blowing on Mayall's "Hideaway," a driving E blues shuffle, and "Steppin' Out," an uptempo boogie blues in G, are examined at length in the pages to come. Both are taken from the 1966 classic *Bluesbreakers with Eric Clapton* album.

Albert King (1923-1992)

A highly prolific and unique performer, Albert King influenced scores of guitarists in both the blues and rock realms, leaving his indelible mark on players such as Jimi Hendrix, Stevie Ray Vaughan, and Eric Clapton. His soul-tinged work for Stax in the 1960s brought him wide acclaim and is highlighted here in excerpts from "Crosscut Saw," a funk blues (in concert A♭), and "Laundromat Blues," a straight-ahead slow blues in B♭. "Crosscut Saw" is notated in A, with the guitar tuned down a half step on all strings. Both songs are taken from his 1967 album *Born Under a Bad Sign*. King himself was an extremely unorthodox left-handed player who usually used a right-handed guitar (often a Gibson Flying V) simply turned upside down without restringing; in other words, the higher pitched strings were on top rather than the bottom, and bends were pulled towards the floor. He also employed a drop-tuning arrangement of B–E–B–E–G♯–C♯, low to high. The looser string tension of this set-up aided his wild, super-wide overbends greatly. For ease of learning and practical application, his work is arranged here in standard tuning (save the half-step drop on "Crosscut Saw") in this book.

B.B. King (b.1925)

Almost certainly the finest ambassador the blues has ever had, B.B. may have slowed down a notch these days but still remains highly active and visible well into his late eighties. King is a powerful singer and iconic guitarist known for his pared-down approach and overall economy, often packing a lot of punch into a simple, vibrato-laden note or two. Over the course of his long career, he has worked with just about everyone who's anyone in the blues world and beyond, plied his trade on stages the world over, and remained an always friendly, welcoming presence to both audiences and up-and-coming young musicians. The simplicity and straightforward nature of his work belies an underlying sophistication and intricacy, tremendous rhythmic thrust, and endless melodicism. B.B.'s style is explored in the pages to come during excerpts from "Five Long Years," an angry and defiant blues shouter in C from 1967's *The Jungle* (also included on a handful of subsequent reissues), and his slow and protracted paean in E to his beloved Gibson ES-335, "Lucille," from the 1968 album of the same name.

John Mayer (b.1977)

The youngest artist featured in these pages is not only a mega-platinum pop star but a tremendous blues guitarist whose skills are often overshadowed by his popularity and matinee-idol status. For those in the know, however, Mayer is acknowledged as the genuine article and an impressive, confident player well-versed in the history and various subgenres of the blues. A spiritual descendant of Stevie Ray Vaughan's, Mayer's mature work now reflects a wide view of the music and often features sophisticated jazz and R&B influences. We examine two live performances in the pages to come: "Blues Intro," an uptempo swinger in C from 2004's *As/Is*, and "Come When I Call," a jazz-tinged, medium-tempo blues in G from his 2008 double CD set *Where the Light Is: John Mayer Live in Los Angeles*. While Mayer is certainly capable of cranking up the overdrive and wailing in a rock-blues vein, these songs take a more traditional, old-school approach and are played with a clean tone and a high degree of refinement and restraint.

Stevie Ray Vaughan (1954–1990)

This legendary Texas guitarist helped to spark a revival of interest in the blues during his reign in the 1980s. His tremendous combination of powerful, emotionally potent vocals, jaw-dropping guitar work, and charismatic stage presence carved a rightful place for him in the pantheon of blues deities. His music evolved steadily and grew markedly more mature with each passing year until his tragic and absurdly early death in 1990 during a helicopter crash. He was a mere 35 years old. In his short career, he collaborated with a wide variety of blues greats, including Albert King, a key influence, in addition to his work with his own band, Double Trouble. The songs selected for this book include the medium tempo E shuffle "Pride and Joy," from the group's 1983 debut album, *Texas Flood*, and the live version of "Texas Flood," a slow blues in G, from the posthumous release *Live at Montreux 1982 & 1985*. More than two decades after his death, Vaughan remains a force to be reckoned with and an inspiration to countless blues guitarists young and old.

The Bigger Picture

The blues, and more specifically blues guitar soloing, is much more than a mere handful of techniques or the process of stringing together a series of licks and phrases. In the pages to come, we'll examine all of the instrument-specific techniques the blues masters employ and illustrate them with multiple examples from their recordings—yes, licks, phrases, riffs, and other vocabulary. It's important to understand and master these techniques as you move towards heightened control of both the instrument and the idiom. The many short examples I have chosen to illustrate them are certainly cool, and you'll likely want to memorize many of them and incorporate them into your own playing. But don't lose sight of the bigger picture(s) along the way. Remember that the blues is first and foremost an emotionally expressive genre and that technical skill, even on a virtuoso level, should be secondary to genuine expression (at least in my view and on the evidence of nearly a century of classic recordings). As we work our way through the book, we'll also learn that a solo is very much like a story or a movie; it has to have an opening, a development, and a climax, and it takes the listener somewhere, even if the only one listening is you. Great soloists almost always demonstrate an instinctive ability to give their improvisations structure, but this instinct is developed over time. Each of the six masters who we will study have been "battle-tested" and paid their dues, so to speak, and each one crafts solos full of great drama, joy, sadness, and all the other emotions along the spectrum.

Finally, concerns of rhythm, rests, and other aspects of phrasing must be considered. The last chapter in this book contains full solos in which structure, emotion, intensity, and rhythmic complexity are all on full display. Take in each page and concept as it comes, but remember that the end result must be more than the sum of the constituent parts, never less.

 (Track 1 is tuning track, standard tuning)

TRACK 1

CHAPTER 2

Articulation Basics: Vibrato, Slides, and More

Some techniques are so essential to blues guitar, and to contemporary guitar playing in general, that it would be nearly impossible to proceed without at least a brief examination of them and the ways in which they are applied. Even if you are well versed in these basic techniques, take the time to look over this chapter; if nothing else, you may pick up a few choice licks and phrases from the examples to follow.

Vibrato

Since the inception of the genre, blues guitarists have sought to emulate the human voice with a variety of techniques, of which *vibrato* is certainly the most basic and commonly applied. Add vibrato to any given note, particularly one that is sustained, by rapidly and repeatedly bending the string up and down a very short distance. Bend the note too far and you will alter the pitch too dramatically, turning your vibrato into a bend, which is a different technique entirely. If you are bending with any finger other than the index finger, line the unused fingers up behind the one playing the note to assist in the process. Vibrato can vary greatly in terms of speed and distance; again, too wide a vibrato will simply make you sound out of tune and perhaps a little goofy.

Let's get things started by taking a look at a few simple phrases using vibrato. The first two are taken from Joe Bonamassa's cover of the Albert Collins classic "Left Overs," an uptempo shuffle in C. The lick below is played over the V–IV–I section of the 12-bar form (measures 9–11) and is simply a repeated C on the B string's 13th fret. Play the note with your 3rd (ring) finger and line up your 1st and 2nd fingers behind it on the 11th and 12th frets, respectively. Keep the vibrato going for the entire phrase. This is one of the those times when hooking your thumb over the top of the neck is actually a good idea and will allow you to stabilize your hand as you "shake" the note over and over again. It's a fitting way to start things off because it not only uses the most basic of techniques but also uses repetition, the simplest "organizational" soloing tool, to great effect.

Vibrato Lick 1 from "Left Overs" *(Joe Bonamassa)*

TRACK 2, 0:00

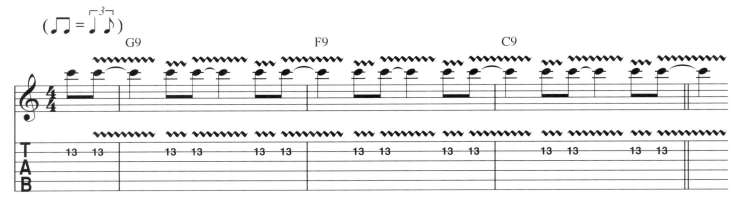

The following phrase, played over the tonic C9 chord during the same solo, also begins on C. This time, though, it's played on the G string's 17th fret. Again, use your 3rd finger, with the others assisting, to apply vibrato during the opening measure. In the second measure, the vibrato is applied to the final note (E♭) by the 2nd (middle) finger, with the 1st finger on the B string's 15th fret providing the assistance.

Vibrato Lick 2 from "Left Overs" *(Joe Bonamassa)*

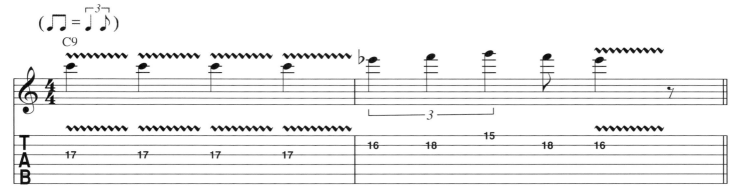

The next example is taken from B.B. King's powerful recording of "Five Long Years." If ever there were a man who could convey so much with a simple vibrato-laden note or two, it's B.B., a minimalist master who puts every over-playing guitar geek to shame with the emotional punch of his playing. This one is also played over a C7 chord and introduces another useful expressive tool: the *rake*. A rake is performed simply by dragging the pick over the strings until you hit your mark (in this case, the E♭ on the high E string's 11th fret), while muting the strings leading up to it with the side of your picking hand. The rake should take almost no actual time and has no real rhythmic value; it's just a percussive "run up" to the note you're shooting for. In this case, the E♭ is to be played by the 1st finger and the C by the 3rd finger on the B string's 13th fret.

Rake and Vibrato from "Five Long Years" *(B.B. King)*

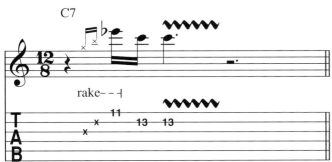

Slides

Let's turn our focus to another simple technique that seeks to emulate the gliding action of the human voice: the *slide*. Slides come in all shapes and sizes, moving up or down a fret or the entire length of the neck. They can connect one note to another or simply fall off or rise up to "nowhere." The only real trick to sliding is to keep enough pressure on the string as your hand moves that the slide is actually audible. You must also be careful to hit your targeted note squarely if called upon to do so and not overshoot or fall short of the mark. Luckily, the short phrase below, taken from John Mayer's "Blues Intro," simply requires us to slide the 1st finger down the low E string a few frets before the note is cut off.

Sliding Phrase from "Blues Intro" *(John Mayer)*

TRACK 3, 0:00

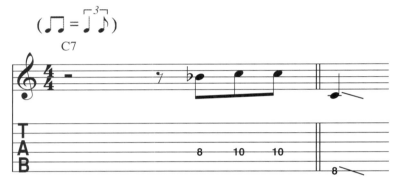

Words and Music by John Mayer
Copyright © 2004 Sony/ATV Music Publishing LLC and Specific Harm Music
All Rights Administered by Sony/ATV Music Publishing LLC, 8 Music Square West, Nashville, TN 37203
International Copyright Secured   All Rights Reserved

The opening measure of Stevie Ray Vaughan's classic "Pride and Joy" begins with a simple slide up the B string from the 3rd fret to the 5th fret E, matching the same pitch on the open 1st string above. Be sure to arch your finger sufficiently to avoid muffling the high E string. Note: Stevie Ray tuned down a half step; however, in this book, for convenience's sake, all examples are shown and played in standard tuning.

Sliding Lick from "Pride and Joy" *(Stevie Ray Vaughan)*

TRACK 3, 0:05

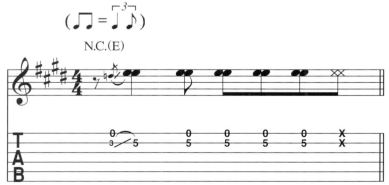

Written by Stevie Ray Vaughan
© 1985 RAY VAUGHAN MUSIC (ASCAP)/Administered by BUG MUSIC
All Rights Reserved   Used by Permission

The short Albert King lick shown below is taken from "Laundromat Blues," which is in the key of B♭. Slide up the B string from a fret or two below with your 1st finger, then use the same finger on the high E string to apply vibrato to the final note.

Slide and Vibrato Combination from "Laundromat Blues" *(Albert King)*

TRACK 3,
0:12

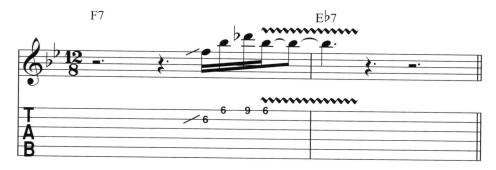

Here's another simple phrase, from Albert King, that combines vibrato and sliding. The source track is "Crosscut Saw," a funky blues in A. Play this one in 3rd position, so that your 1st finger plays all 3rd fret notes and adds vibrato to the G notes in both measures. The slide in measure 2 should be performed with the ring finger. This is a grace note slide, meaning that the little D that's upstemmed in the notation should be heard but not have any real, quantifiable rhythmic value. Note: Albert used a dropped alterate tuning; however, in this book, for conveniences sake, all examples are shown and play in standard tuning.

Slide and Vibrato Combination from "Crosscut Saw" *(Albert King)*

TRACK 3,
0:23

Hammer-ons and Pull-offs

Two more essential techniques that should be familiar to all but the greenest of guitarists are *hammer-ons* and *pull-offs*. They are employed extensively in all genres and can add a great deal of legato smoothness to any given phrase. A hammer-on simply requires the player to pick a note and then bring a finger down on the same string with enough force to sound another higher pitch. If the initial note is not an open string, the fretting hand finger playing it will nearly always remain in place on the string while the hammering finger does its job. If you are just learning to perform hammer-ons, keep the name of the technique in mind while you work on it; it's indicative of the amount of force needed to sound the hammered pitch clearly. The higher your guitar's action (string height), the harder this technique will be.

A pull-off is basically the reverse technique; you pick a given note, then pull down and off the string to sound a lower note. If the lower note is not an open string, the finger playing it must already be in place before the pulling-off process begins. Hammer-ons and pull-offs should not be used indiscriminately or to mask a lack of traditional picking ability. That's not to say that you need to spend a lot of time thinking about how and where to employ them, but don't use them as a crutch or to play a phrase that is intended to be picked normally. As an experiment, try playing the hammer-on/pull-off phrases that follow by picking every note to hear just how much they can alter the sound of a melodic line.

In the short lick from B.B. King's "Lucille," shown below, pick only the G notes on the high E string, then lift your 3rd finger off the string while pulling towards the floor slightly to sound the 12th fret E played by your 1st finger.

Pull-off Lick from "Lucille" *(B.B. King)*

**TRACK 4,
0:00**

The following excerpt from Eric Clapton's famous solo on "Steppin' Out" combines sliding, vibrato, and a hammer-on. It's extremely simple but shows just how much impact these expressive tools can have on even as little as two or three notes. Use your 2nd finger for the G string slide and vibrato in measure 1, and then hammer-on from your 1st finger to your 3rd finger on the B string in measure 2.

Slide/Vibrato/Hammer-on Combo from "Steppin' Out" *(Eric Clapton)*

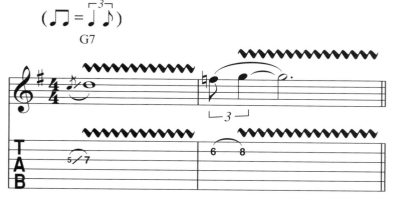

The final four examples in this chapter are all taken from Joe Bonamassa's "Left Overs." The solo-opener below begins with a D string hammer-on from the 1st to the 3rd finger, followed by a G string pull-off from the 3rd finger back to the 1st finger. In traditional blues/rock fashion, the pinky is passed over here in lieu of a 3rd (ring) finger extension. In this case, it makes a lot of sense because the pinky often isn't particularly effective for pulling off, although strength and agility can and should be developed in this digit. In measure 2, rake across the strings and play the B♭ with your 2nd finger. Albert Collins, the original composer and performer of this song, was a particularly percussive, slashing player with a penetrating telecaster tone; Joe gets more than a little bit of his vibe on this solo by employing rakes, heavy vibrato, and a similar rhythmic approach.

Hammer/Pull/Rake Combo from "Left Overs" *(Joe Bonamassa)*

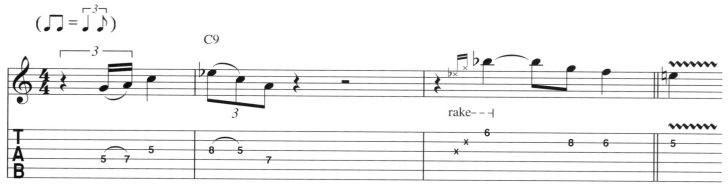

The lick below is played over the IV chord (F9) and begins with a grace note hammer-on from the 1st to the 3rd finger. Be sure to lay the vibrato on thick during the sustained C on the high E string. Later in the 1st measure, play three notes on a single pick stroke by hammering on and pulling off from your 1st to your 2nd finger and back on the B string. In measure 2, your 3rd finger should play both the slide and the 10th fret F on the G string that ends the lick.

Hammer-on/Pull-off Combo from "Left Overs" *(Joe Bonamassa)*

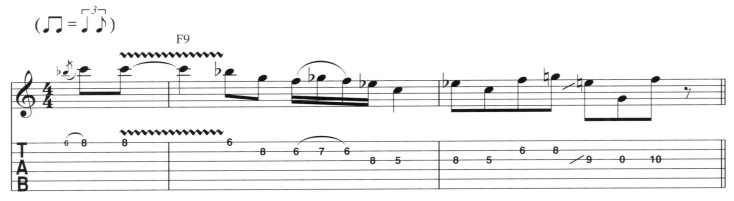

The next lick is played entirely above the 12th fret and begins with a quick hammer-on from the 2nd to the 3rd finger. After playing the B♭ on the G string's 15th fret with your 1st finger, shift positions quickly so the D string pull-off is performed by your 3rd finger. The 17th fret notes in the 2nd measure should be played by the 4th (pinky) finger. Near the end of the phrase, slide up the D string from the 15th to the 17th fret with your 3rd finger and finish things off with same hammer-on that began the lick.

Combination Phrase from "Left Overs" *(Joe Bonamassa)*

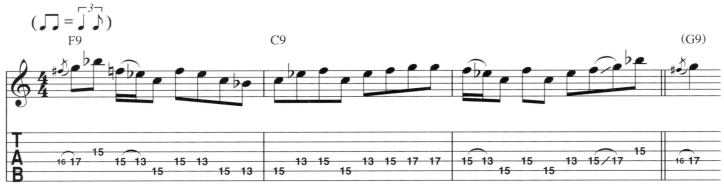

The final example in this chapter begins in the same way as the previous one: with a 2nd to 3rd finger hammer-on high up on the D string. In the 2nd measure, use your 3rd finger to slide quickly down from the 17th to the 15th fret and then pull off to your 1st finger. One of the cool things about this phrase is the use of both repetition and displacement, hallmarks of Albert Collins' style. What is meant by the latter is that the same melodic idea (the combination of the grace note G and B♭ above) is repeated but begins on a different beat each time—first on the downbeat, next on the "2-and," then on beat 4, and finally on the "1-and" of measure 2.

Hammer-on Lick with Displacement from "Left Overs" *(Joe Bonamassa)*

TRACK 4, 0:34

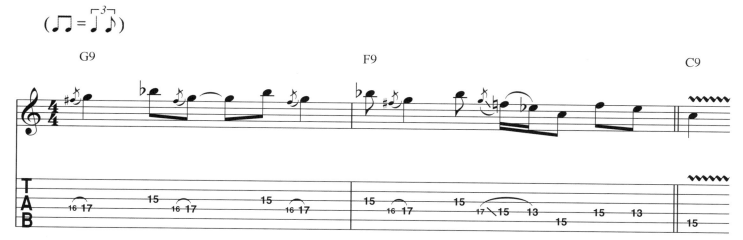

CHAPTER 3

The Major and Minor Pentatonic Scales: the Raw Materials of Blues Soloing

The core "source materials" for soloing over the blues are the pentatonic scales. Almost every guitarist reading these pages will be familiar with the minor pentatonic scale, but many either won't know the major pentatonic scale or will not yet be comfortable with either the fingerings or applications for it. We'll review both scales in a variety of positions and fingerings momentarily, but first here is a very general rule to follow regarding their application: the minor pentatonic scale with the same root as the home key of the song you're playing can be used over the entire 12-bar form. For instance, in a G blues, a G minor pentatonic scale will work beautifully. This is the obvious choice and one we all should be completely familiar with. When adding in the major pentatonic, the following "rule" applies: match the root of the scale to the chord you're playing. For instance, over the I chord (G), use the G major pentatonic. Over the IV (C), use the C major pentatonic, and over the V (D), use the D major pentatonic. Any of these choices can and should be combined with the G minor pentatonic scale to create a richer, more sophisticated sound than just wailing on a single pentatonic scale (although that does have a place to be sure!). One approach favored by many great blues soloists is to simply play the G minor pentatonic scale over the whole form, but switch to the D major pentatonic scale over the D chord in measure 10 only, creating a momentary contrast that quickly reverts back to conventional minor pentatonic licks or "turnaround" phrases through measures 11 and 12. Also remember that rules are made to be broken, but you should master playing within these boundaries before choosing to shrug them off. After examining the fingerings to follow, we will check out some examples of the blues greats using these scales in a variety of ways, both individually and in combination.

Let's start with the more familiar minor pentatonic scale, which uses the following scale degrees: 1–♭3–4–5–♭7. In the key of G, this would be G–B♭–C–D–F; in the key of A, it would be A–C–D–E–G. The "blues scale" is a variation of the minor pentatonic that adds the flatted 5th degree to the scale (D♭ in the key of G, E♭ in the key of A). These are indicated in the diagram by the notes in parentheses and can be added or omitted as dictated by the player's individual tastes. Be sure to familiarize yourself with both the traditional minor pentatonic scale and the blues scale variation. The "blue note" can be fairly dissonant, so it should be used with a good deal of discretion.

All of the following diagrams will be in the key of G, but each of these fingerings are movable forms that can be transposed to any key you need. Learn to play them all over the neck and in all keys so you're not lost when you have to play in, say, D♭!

The tonics are circled in each diagram. Here's the most common blues scale fingering by far:

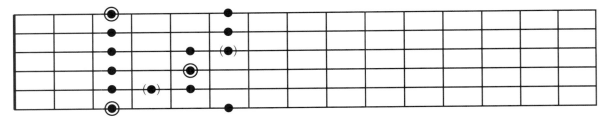

Here's a common variation beginning on the middle (2nd) finger:

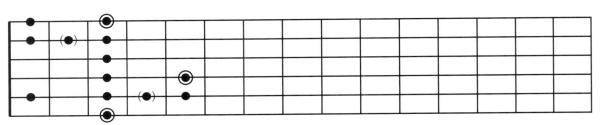

And here is an extremely useful variation beginning on the A string rather than on the low E string:

10th Fret

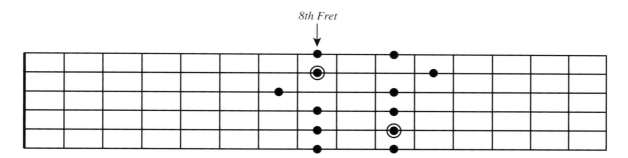

Even if you know only these three variations, you will have a lot of possibilities before you. You can begin down on the 3rd fret, playing from the first two fingerings, then climb to the 10th fret of the A string to play the higher G minor pentatonic scale, finally climbing all the way to the 15th fret for the initial scale fingerings up an octave. Changing registers is a great way to build intensity and excitement in a solo and work toward a climax!

Next are the minor pentatonic fingerings beginning on each scale degree that isn't the tonic. The first starts on the flatted 3rd (B♭ in the key of G). Start with your 2nd finger.

5th Fret

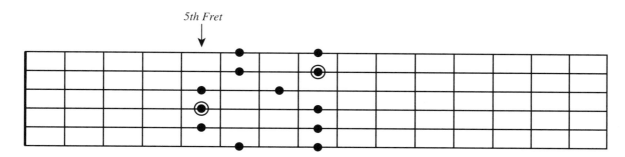

Next is the G minor pentatonic scale beginning on the 4th (C). This one should also begin with the 2nd finger.

8th Fret

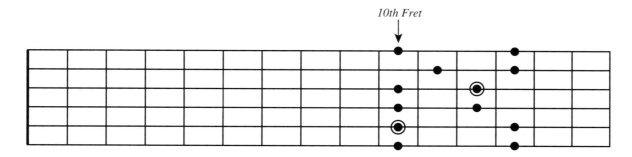

Here's the G minor pentatonic scale starting from the 5th degree (D). This one starts with the index (1st) finger.

10th Fret

Finally, the diagram below shows the same scale beginning on the ♭7th (F). Start this one with the middle (2nd) finger.

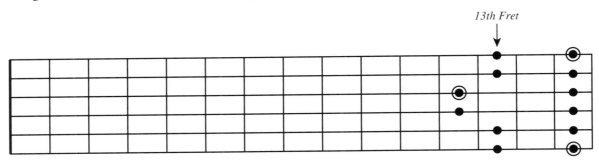

13th Fret

Once you've got these under your fingers and memorized, begin learning them in all 12 keys. That may sound like a lot, but if you can accomplish it you'll be ready for nearly any situation. Narrow your work down a bit by starting with the most commonly encountered keys (A, E, D, etc.) and add in the others as time goes by. Not only will you be able to approach any key from any area of the neck, you'll really start to unlock the fretboard and get away from "box" playing, in which you're trapped in one position. As we work our way through this book, you'll see the masters move around freely from position to position, often in the course of a single lick.

Now let's turn out attention to the major pentatonic scale, which includes the tonic (1), 2nd, 3rd, 5th, and 6th scale degrees (G, A, B, D, E in the key of G). As you play the most common fingering below, starting with the 2nd finger, you'll find that it's identical to the minor pentatonic scale beginning on the flatted 3rd. This is because the two scales are basically modes of each other, a minor 3rd (three frets) apart: the G major pentatonic scale has the same notes as the E minor pentatonic scale; the G minor pentatonic scale has the same notes as the B♭ major pentatonic scale. E is the relative minor of G major; B♭ is the relative major of G minor.

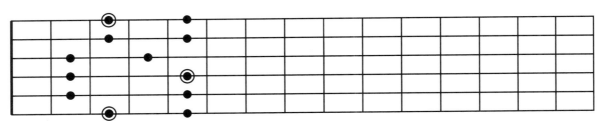

Next is the same scale shown in a popular alternate fingering beginning with the 1st finger. This one is a little more "open" and allows for easier positional shifts to the higher frets.

5th Fret

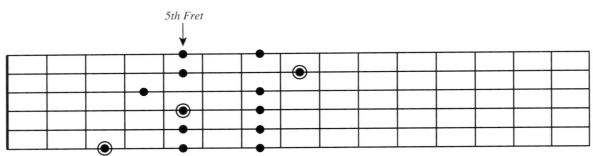

The diagram below shows the G major pentatonic scale beginning on the A string rather than the low E string. You may want to begin this one on your 1st finger and then simply slide up two frets and finish out the scale without further shifting.

12th Fret

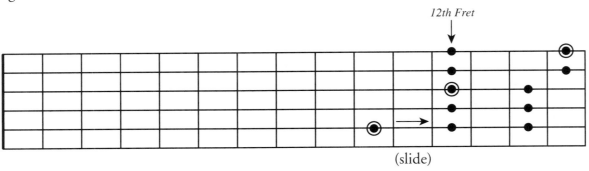

(slide)

Now let's go through the various fingerings of the G major pentatonic scale beginning on notes other than the tonic. Here is the same scale beginning on the 2nd (A). Once again the tonics (G) are circled to help you get oriented.

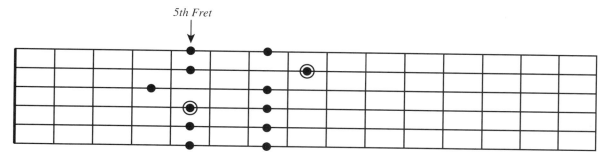

Here's the G major pentatonic scale starting on the 3rd (B). Begin with your 1st finger.

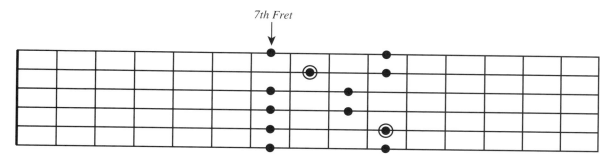

Next is the same scale beginning on the 5th (D). This fingering starts with the 2nd finger.

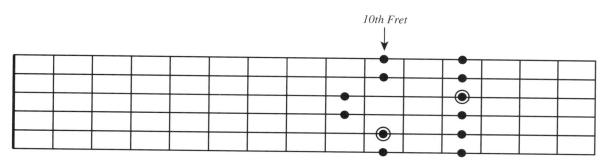

Finally, here's the G major pentatonic scale beginning on the 6th degree (E), with the 1st finger. As you can see, it's identical to the E minor pentatonic scale. Any time you are soloing over an E minor chord, you can use a G major pentatonic scale; conversely, you can play an E minor pentatonic scale over a G chord in the same way.

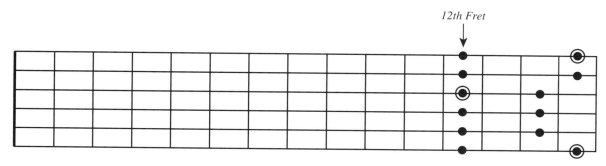

Learn all of the above fingerings and begin to transpose them to various keys. Take your time, as it's a lot of work and a lot of fingerings. Before you know it, though, they'll be under your fingers, and your understanding and command of the fretboard will have increased exponentially. Think about it: if you had all of the major and minor pentatonic fingerings down pat, you could play a blues in any key, in any position, and in any region of the neck, move up and down freely, and never be lost or be locked in the "blues box" again. You'd never have to cling desperately to the root on the low E string to keep yourself oriented. Develop your command and understanding of these fingerings patiently and you'll elevate your playing and break out of the limited approach so many amateur blues guitarists find themselves stuck with.

Now let's take a look at some short pentatonic licks played by the masters. As we work our way through the book, pay attention to which scales and fingerings they are using and how they combine them or move from one to another. I'll point them out as we go as well. Needless to say, there will be *a lot* of pentatonics from here on out, so this chapter and the licks to follow are really just an introduction to the subject. Let's start with something easy, like this short phrase from Albert King's "Laundromat Blues," which uses notes from the B♭ minor pentatonic scale in the most common fingering. The 1st finger should play all the 6th fret notes; you may use your pinky for the 9th fret notes or stretch with your 3rd finger as many blues and rock guitarists choose to do.

Minor Pentatonic Lick from "Laundromat Blues" *(Albert King)*

Here's another one from Albert King in the key of A. This lick is played over an E7 chord but would work equally well over A7 or D7. This is basically the high end of the A string minor pentatonic scale fingering. Play it in 3rd position so that your 1st finger takes all the 3rd fret notes.

Minor Pentatonic Lick from "Crosscut Saw" *(Albert King)*

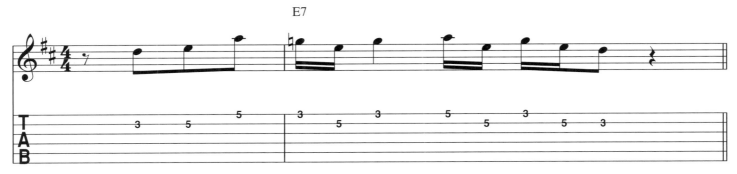

Now let's check out a few simple phrases played by B.B. King. The first is taken from "Five Long Years" and uses the C minor pentatonic scale over the IV chord (F7). Play it in 11th position so that your 1st finger takes the 11th fret notes and your 3rd finger plays the notes on the 13th fret. This is basically at the top of the second fingering shown for the minor pentatonic scale (beginning on the minor 3rd, not the root).

Minor Pentatonic Lick from "Five Long Years" *(B.B. King)*

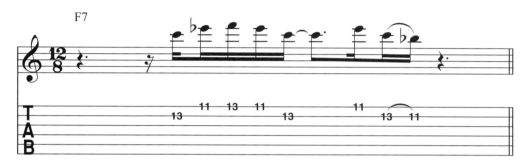

Let's move onto B.B.'s classic "Lucille," a slow E blues in which he talks at length about his relationship with his beloved Gibson ES-335. This is straight-up blues "box" playing in the 12th fret E minor pentatonic scale; the real challenge here is getting the rhythms right. The bracketed 4s indicate that four notes are fit into the duration of three. This is complicated somewhat in the first grouping because the first of the four notes isn't played but is instead a rest. Take a listen to the recording if you're having trouble with this one; the line has an almost conversational feel (Lucille is "chatting" with B.B.), but rest assured the rhythms are precise and always exactly as intended.

Minor Pentatonic Lick from "Lucille" *(B.B. King)*

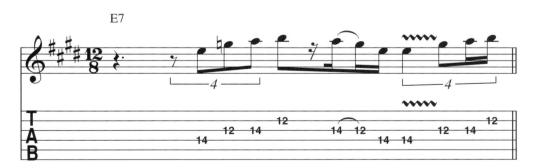

The next two examples are taken from the same song and are played over the IV chord (A7). In each, B.B. combines notes from the E minor pentatonic scale with the C♯ taken from the E major pentatonic (or A major pentatonic, if you prefer—C♯ can be found in both scales). The important thing here is that, by mixing this C♯ in with the more familiar minor pentatonic tones, he is "acknowledging" the A7 chord by playing its major 3rd. It's such a small change and yet it has a big impact and changes the sound of the line dramatically. Simply wailing on the E minor pentatonic scale over every chord would have a totally different sound and vibe, and ultimately a lot less harmonic and melodic interest. It's a minor tweak that really brings out the sound of the A7 chord.

Pentatonic Combination 1 from "Lucille" *(B.B. King)*

Pentatonic Combination 2 from "Lucille" *(B.B. King)*

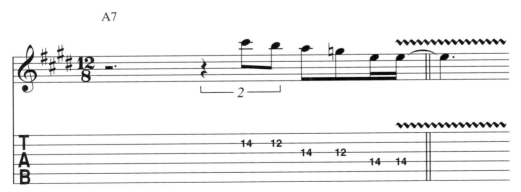

Let's move on to a few short licks by John Mayer. The first two are from his live performance of "Blues Intro," an old-school, swinging blues shuffle in C. This one is taken from the C major pentatonic fingering beginning on the A string's 3rd fret and begins with a hammer-on/pull-off combination (pick just once for the first three notes). As is often the case, the 3rd finger is charged with this task.

Major Pentatonic Lick from "Blues Intro" *(John Mayer)*

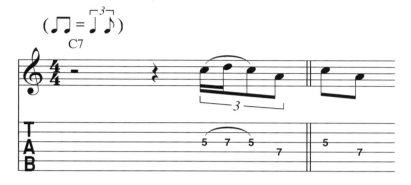

The lick below immediately follows the one above and combines C major and minor pentatonic scales nicely. Begin by hammering on from your 1st to your 2nd finger and stay in position until sliding down the A string from the 10th to the 8th fret with your 3rd finger at the end of the initial measure. Your 1st finger should perform the final downwards slide. The inclusion of both the major and minor 3rds of the C7 chord (E and E♭, respectively) is a classic sound in blues vocabulary.

Pentatonic Combination from "Blues Intro" *(John Mayer)*

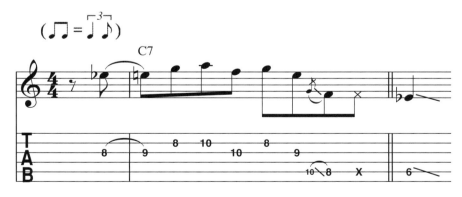

The lick in G below, from "Come When I Call," also puts the minor and major 3rds of a dominant chord in close proximity (B♭ and B of the G9 chord). There's a definite jazziness to these sounds that's quite different from the more blues-rock feeling of the straight minor pentatonic scale. Begin this one with your 3rd finger and play the double stop (two notes at the same time) on beat 4 of measure 1 by using your 1st finger to barre the G and B strings. Then hammer on from the G string's 3rd fret to the 4th fret with your 2nd finger.

Pentatonic Combination from "Come When I Call" *(John Mayer)*

The next lick begins Joe Bonamassa's blistering rendition of "Blues Deluxe" and combines C major and minor pentatonic scales in a classic bit of blues vocabulary. The pick-up includes another minor and major 3rd combo (E♭ and E). In the full measure, the minor 3rd is played again on the high E string and is bent upwards slightly (just give the string a little push towards your face; the subject of bending will be examined extensively in the following chapter). The ♭7th of the C7 chord (B♭) that ends the lick also gives a bit of edge to the (mostly) major pentatonic sound. By now, you should be noticing that the combination of the two scales is never done haphazardly and that certain groupings are both common and particularly tasty.

Pentatonic Combination from "Blues Deluxe" *(Joe Bonamassa)*

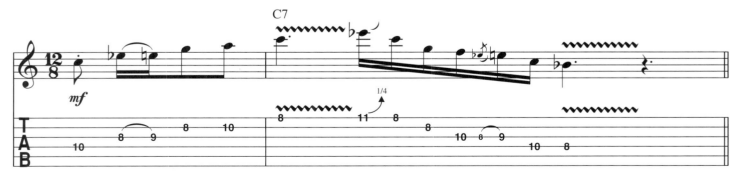

The following lick from "Left Overs" is strictly C minor pentatonic—until the inclusion of the A (the major 6th) at the end of the phrase. This simple addition, borrowed from the C major pentatonic scale, changes the vibe of the line quite a bit, giving it a sunnier, happier feeling. Take heed: even if you play minor pentatonic scales 95% of the time, a strategically placed major note here or there will have a huge impact.

Minor Pentatonic Lick with Major 6th from "Left Overs" *(Joe Bonamassa)*

TRACK 15

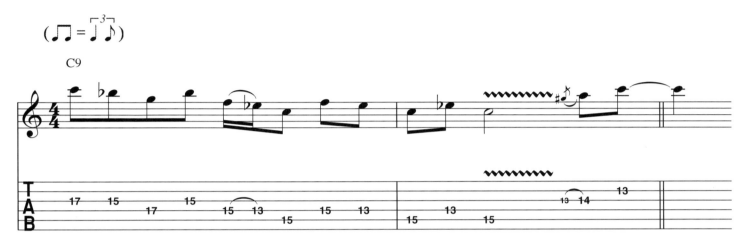

Our final example in this chapter is the opening melodic break from "Left Overs," an eight-bar phrase that combines C major and minor pentatonic scales extensively. Rest assured we will continue to examine these scales both separately and in combination during the remainder of this book. In the meantime, start this one in 3rd position, hammering on from your 1st finger to your 3rd finger, then shift up two frets to 5th position at the end of measure 2. Along the way, C minor pentatonic notes are embellished by the major 6th (A), major 3rd (E), and the raised 5th (G♯), a chromatic passing tone used to connect G to A.

Intro Lick from "Left Overs" *(Joe Bonamassa)*

TRACK 16

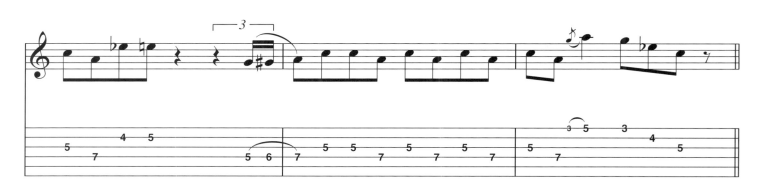

CHAPTER 4

String Bending

Perhaps no single technique is more essential to modern blues soloing than *string bending.* Since the style's inception, guitarists have pushed and pulled the strings, raising pitches and bringing them back down, in an effort to simulate the cries, moans, and smooth glissandos of the human voice. As the genre developed and players became increasingly sophisticated and technically accomplished, the art of bending followed suit and became more vital, multi-faceted, and ingrained in the collective vocabulary. There are a wide variety of bending techniques to learn, so let's jump right into it by examining the ways in which the master soloists put them to use.

Our first example is taken from B.B. King's "Five Long Years" and immediately shines a light on two of the most important aspects of string bending. First, bend in tune and to a specific pitch. There are times, seldom indeed, that you may want to bend wildly and randomly to create an odd effect. For the most part, however, your bends should be hitting a target squarely. You may want to play the targeted pitch before attempting a bending lick to be sure you are actually sounding it accurately. The lick below, in the key of C, finds B.B. bending the 4th (F) to the 5th (G) before releasing the bend back down, pulling off to the minor 3rd (E♭), and ending on the tonic (C). The numeral "1" in the tab indicates the bend is a distance of one whole step (from F to G).

The second key bending "rule" is to use non-bending fingers to help the push by lining up on the string in question behind the bending finger. In this phrase, the 3rd finger bends the high E string with the assistance of the 1st and 2nd fingers behind it. This makes pushing the string that much easier to accomplish, particularly if you have heavy gauge strings, high action, or are bending a lower pitched, heavier string. Give it a shot.

Bending Lick from "Five Long Years" *(B.B. King)*

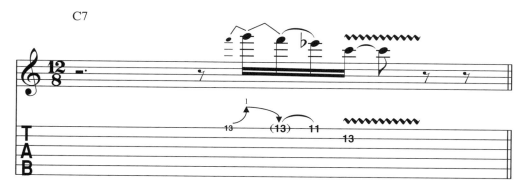

Guitarists are told from the beginning to play with arched fingers, particularly when playing chords, to avoid dampening strings and preventing all notes from ringing clearly (think of the arch required of your 3rd finger on the B string in a basic open D chord to avoid deadening the high E string above). The same technique is important while bending; if you allow your bending finger to straighten, rather than remain arched, you'll sap yourself of all your pushing strength and struggle to hit your targets accurately (or to hold bends out for long durations). In the next lick, by Albert King, the 3rd finger bends the G string up a whole step and then plays the unbent note, but there's an important distinction from the previous example: we don't release the bend and hear it descend back down (from F to E♭). Instead, simply bend up to the F, then play the unbent note quickly after without making the release audible. Once again, you should use your 3rd finger (the primary bending finger by far), with the 1st and 2nd fingers lined up behind it to assist, and keep your fingers arched the entire time; the exception is the very last note, which may be played by flattening your 1st finger into a barre as you jump from the G to the high E string. The song is in the key of B♭, and the lick, played over the IV chord (E♭7), is taken from the B♭ minor pentatonic scale.

Bending Lick 1 from "Laundromat Blues" *(Albert King)*

In the next lick, the 3rd finger once again bends E♭ up a whole step to F, raising the 4th to the 5th degree of a B♭ minor pentatonic scale. The main difference here is in the rhythm; the unbent tone should be heard clearly, and we arrive at the targeted F note an eighth note later. In the previous example, the bend occurred immediately and took up no measurable time; the note was simply struck and bent. Here, strive for rhythmic accuracy and clear delineation of both bent and unbent pitches.

Bending Lick 2 from "Laundromat Blues" *(Albert King)*

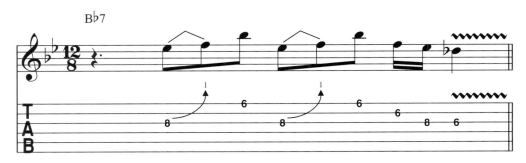

Let's stick with Albert King for the moment but turn our attention to some licks from "Crosscut Saw," a classic blues in A. Our first example from this tune is definitely the easiest; it's a simple quarter step bend on the high E string, meaning the bent note (C) should be raised only slightly—not even far enough to hit C♯ a half step above. This is one of those times when you don't really have a target tone in mind but simply give the note a little push for effect.

Quarter Step Bend from "Crosscut Saw" *(Albert King)*

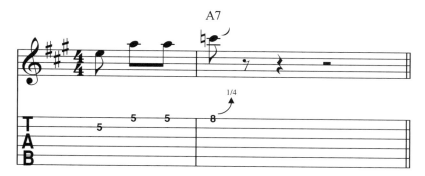

In the next example, the same note (C) is bent, but this time it's raised a whole step to D in an eighth note rhythm. Your 3rd finger should do the bending and play all other 8th fret notes, while your 1st finger takes the notes on the 5th fret. This is straight-ahead A minor pentatonic playing in the 5th position "box." Remember to use your 1st and 2nd fingers to assist in the bending process; again, the lowering of the high E string back down to C should not be audible in this phrase.

Whole Step Bending Lick from "Crosscut Saw" *(Albert King)*

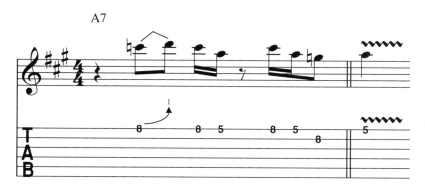

The next lick includes both whole and half step bends. Once again, the unbent pitch is C, but this time it's raised to both C♯ and D. Play both of these notes (on the 9th and 10th frets of the high E string, respectively) before attempting the lick to be sure you know exactly how your bending targets should sound. We're stepping up the difficulty level quite a bit here, and it's essential that you hit the pitches accurately to make this phrase sound the way it should. Falling short or overshooting your targets will quickly turn this into an amateurish mess.

Combination Bending Lick from "Crosscut Saw" *(Albert King)*

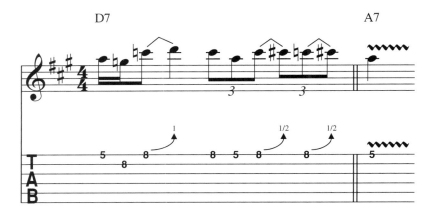

We'll get back to Albert King shortly, but let us now turn our attention to Joe Bonamassa and two short licks from "Left Overs." The first is a classic move played way up on the 18th frets of the B and high E strings; the bend is executed by the 3rd finger, while the 4th finger takes the B♭ above. The B string is bent twice (don't hold out the initial bend), and the release of the first bend should be silent. After the second bend, hold the targeted pitch (G), then apply vibrato. Don't start shaking the note until you've hit your pitch accurately—trying to add vibrato to an out-of-tune bend will just make things even messier. It's a matter of a split second, but it's critical that you get your bend in tune before applying any vibrato.

Bend with Vibrato from "Left Overs" *(Joe Bonamassa)*

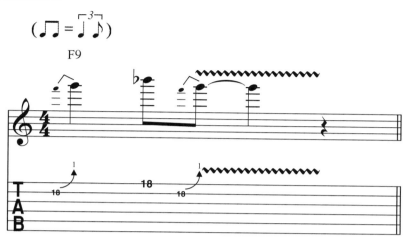

The next lick is played in 13th position, with the 3rd finger yet again doing all the bending. The notes are taken from the C major pentatonic scale (C–D–E–G–A) and are played over measures 9–10 of a 12-bar C blues. This one is a little different because in each measure the whole step bend is released back to its unbent position audibly. In the second measure, the release is followed by a pull-off to the 1st finger.

Bend and Release from "Left Overs" *(Joe Bonamassa)*

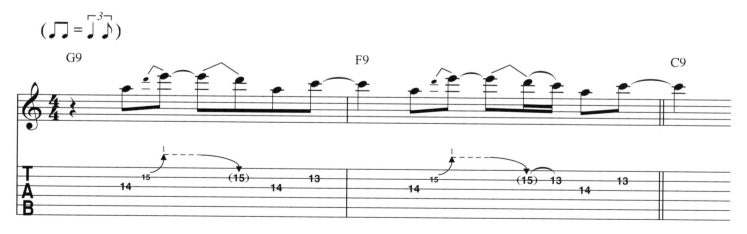

Here's a tricky little phrase from B.B. King. The 12/8 rhythms are somewhat intricate, so be sure you know exactly where in the measure each note falls. The lick is somewhat "conversational" and is a response to his vocal but nonetheless is very precisely placed in the measure. The line is additionally challenging because the initial bend is played by the 1st finger alone, without assistance from other fingerings to aid in the push. This is relatively uncommon because of the strength required and the overall awkwardness of the technique. Make sure you raise the B a full step up to C♯. Stay in 12th position throughout until reaching down with your 1st finger to grab the C♯ on the D string that ends the lick.

1st Finger Bending Lick from "Lucille" *(B.B. King)*

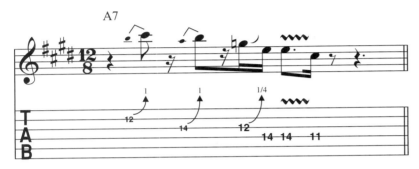

The next two examples are taken from John Mayer's uptempo swinger "Blues Intro" and feature a number of subtly challenging maneuvers. In the first, we begin with a 3rd finger whole step bend and continue in measure 2 by sliding up the high E string from the 11th to the 13th fret with the 1st finger. Follow up by switching positions quickly to grab the C on the B string with your 2nd finger and finish out the phrase with a 1st finger, half step bend. Make sure you hit the E natural (the major 3rd of the C7 chord) cleanly here.

Position Shifting Lick from "Blues Intro" *(John Mayer)*

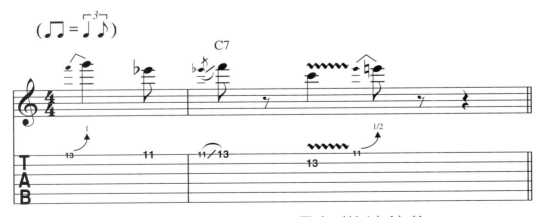

The lick below is played in 13th position, with the 3rd finger reaching out to the 16th fret to perform all the bends and the 2nd finger grabbing the A on the G string in measure 1. This one really demands precision bending, as the E♭ is raised to E natural on three separate occasions and is twice followed by an F above. The second measure begins with three chromatic notes in quick succession: E♭, E, and F. Play these pitches by fretting normally before attempting the lick to give yourself a guideline of exactly how each note should sound; then nail them squarely!

Half Step Bending Lick from "Blues Intro" *(John Mayer)*

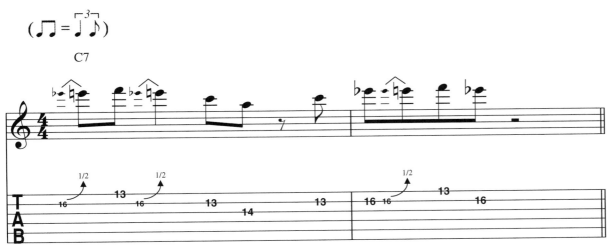

Words and Music by John Mayer
Copyright © 2004 Sony/ATV Music Publishing LLC and Specific Harm Music
All Rights Administered by Sony/ATV Music Publishing LLC, 8 Music Square West, Nashville, TN 37203
International Copyright Secured   All Rights Reserved

Let's jump around a bit now and explore some of the more advanced bending techniques employed by each of our blues greats. We'll look at plenty of Stevie Ray Vaughan stuff as we work our way through these pages, but let's start with something easy from the intro to "Pride and Joy." In this lick, the repeated Bs on the high E string remain stationary (unbent) while the B string is bent below. This technique is often called an "oblique bend." Use your 1st finger to play the Bs and your 2nd finger to do the bending on the G note. Note that we are raising the Gs only a quarter step so don't push them all the way up to G♯. Another new wrinkle below is that each bend is held and struck a second time before we re-bend the string again. This one is pretty easy to pull off; in some of the examples to follow, you'll really need to develop your finger strength to raise the string and hold it, in tune, for longer durations.

Oblique Bend from "Pride and Joy" *(Stevie Ray Vaughan)*

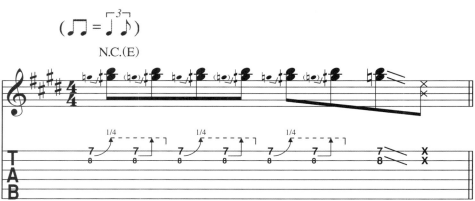

Let's go back to John Mayer for the moment and explore the idea of two-string combination bending a bit further. The next two examples feature unison bends, in which the upper note (in this case, C on the high E string) remains stationary while the lower note (B♭ on the B string) is bent upwards to match it. Unison bends not only sound super cool but are also an excellent barometer for accuracy in intonation, because if you fall short or go past the higher pitch, you'll hear it; and it won't be pretty! In each of the next two licks, the 1st finger should play the Cs while the 3rd finger performs the pitch-matching bend on the B string. In measure 2 there are some tasty double stops (another subject we will look at in deeper detail as we move along) in which 1st and 3rd finger barres are used to play two strings at once. For the final double stop, barre the G and B strings with your 1st finger and perform the G string hammer-on with your 2nd finger.

Unison Bending Lick 1 from "Blues Intro" *(John Mayer)*

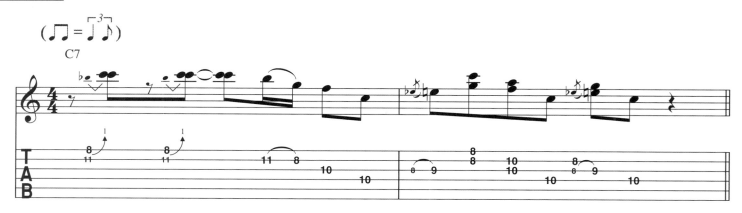

The lick below elaborates on the previous idea and demonstrates how the re-use or re-imagining of previous material can be a valuable tool in a soloist's arsenal. Much of what is included here appeared in the preceding excerpt but is now played over the V (G9), IV (F9), and I chords (C7) rather than just over the tonic. Mayer also employs rhythmic displacement to great effect; the unison bends that were played on the "1-and" and "2-and" before are now placed on the "4-and" as well as the "3-and" and "4-and" of measure 2. Displacing the bends shifts the entire phrase over in each measure—a tricky bit of phrase manipulation to be sure. Don't gloss over these two concepts. Rhythmic displacement and re-use of material (particular over a variety of chords) can take your soloing to a whole new level that has nothing to do with technique. Rather than using these ideas in a contrived way, play around with them in the practice room until they start to become instinctive and trickle into your playing more subconsciously. This is something that happens with nearly all techniques and concepts if given enough of a chance.

Unison Bending Lick 2 from "Blues Intro" *(John Mayer)*

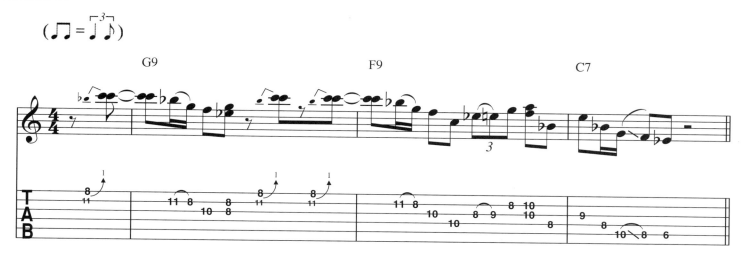

Our final bending example from this song features another new technique: bending two strings simultaneously with one finger. In general, when a single string is bent, the neighboring string should be pushed out of the way by the bending finger if necessary to complete the bend (in no case should the bending finger go under the neighboring string). In this lick, however, the 3rd finger bends the high E string and catches the B string at the same time while bending (and releasing). Note that the second string is bent one and a quarter steps, which is slightly farther than the first string. This is a tricky technique to be sure, so give it a little time. Make sure your pick actually hits both strings and roll your 3rd fingertip slightly towards the B string to ensure you actually cover it sufficiently.

Two String Bend from "Blues Intro" *(John Mayer)*

TRACK 31

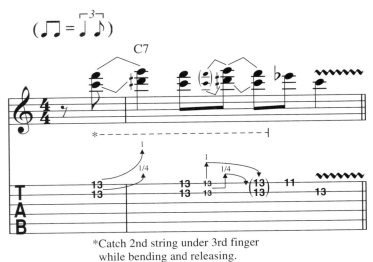

*Catch 2nd string under 3rd finger
while bending and releasing.

Here's a lick from Joe Bonamassa using the same finger to bend the same two strings at the same fret, but there are two big differences here as well: both strings are bent approximately the same distance (a whole step), and you must re-bend the strings a full 12 times! As you perform the initial bend, push the high E string towards the B string and catch it under your fingertip instantaneously; this maneuver must be completed before your pick hits the strings. Once you have both strings firmly under your fingertip, press down sufficiently throughout the lick to keep them there as you bend up repeatedly. Again, this is a bit advanced, so take your time as you work on this technique.

Two String Bend from "Blues Deluxe" *(Joe Bonamassa)*

TRACK 32

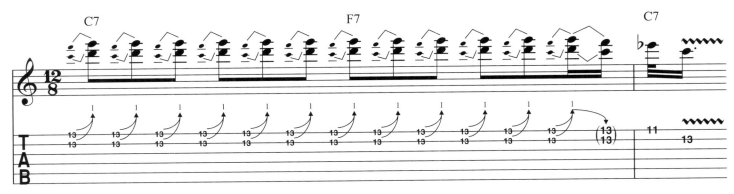

Let us now turn our attention to Old Slowhand, the great Eric Clapton, and examine the ways he puts these techniques (and others) to use in excerpts from "Hide Away" and "Steppin' Out." In the following lick from the former song, the B string is bent and held with the 3rd finger. Begin by pushing the F# up a whole step to G# and striking it six times. On beat 3, Clapton pulls off a few subtly tricky maneuvers: he first bends up a whole step, then pushes it just a tad further (to somewhere between G# and A), and then performs an overbend to A (a full step and a half). To add to the difficulty level, the latter two bends are *pre-bends*, meaning they are raised to the specified pitches before they are picked. Pre-bends can be particularly difficult at first because you have to know exactly how far to push the string to reach your desired pitch without hearing it; variable tension from string to string and even fret to fret adds to the challenge. Every guitar will play a little differently too, so pre-bending the B string on a Telecaster will demand a different touch than doing the same thing on a Les Paul. This is one of those times when you will again want to play the targeted pitches before attempting the lick to hear exactly how the notes you're aiming for should sound. Don't be content to merely approximate this one; do it right and hit the G#, A, and in-between note as well.

Pre-bend and Overbend Lick from "Hide Away" *(Eric Clapton)*

By Freddie King and Sonny Thompson
Copyright © 1961 by Fort Knox Music Inc. and Bug Music-Trio Music Company
Copyright Renewed
International Copyright Secured   All Rights Reserved
Used by Permission

The short lick below kicks off with a unison bend, in which the B and high E strings are struck simultaneously. The B string is bent up a whole step to match the G played on the high E string above it. Since the targeted pitch and the stationary pitch are one and the same, it should be easy to hear if you are in tune or not. Use your 3rd finger for both the initial bend and the final bend, which also raises F to G on the B string but omits the high E string note above it.

Unison Bend from "Steppin' Out" (*Eric Clapton*)

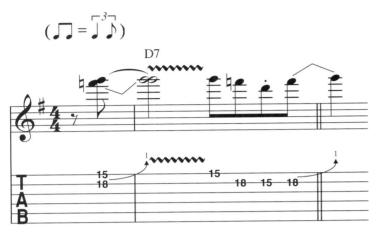

In the following lick, one note (B♭ on the high E string's 18th fret) is bent repeatedly up to C, B, and finally, up a quarter step (between B♭ and B). Use your 3rd finger throughout. This is one that should be played very slowly after carefully noting the exact sound of each targeted pitch. By all means work this one up to full speed, but the main reason for its inclusion here is as an exercise in bending accuracy. Slow it way down and hit each pitch right on the nose before trying it at full speed.

Whole, Half, and Quarter Step Bends from "Steppin' Out" (*Eric Clapton*)

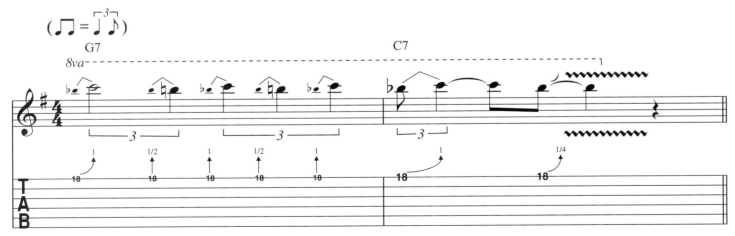

In this lick from "Hide Away," played over the IV chord (A7 in an E blues), Clapton bends the D on the B string's 15th fret four times—twice in rhythm and twice as a pre-bend. It's a nice opportunity to use both techniques side by side. The fact that each pre-bend is preceded by a standard bend makes the former a bit easier; you will already know how the targeted pitch should sound and exactly how far to push the string to hit that target. Stay in 12th position throughout the phrase, using your 3rd finger for each bend and for the final vibrato-laden E note on the D string's 14th fret.

Bend and Pre-bend Combination from "Hide Away" *(Eric Clapton)*

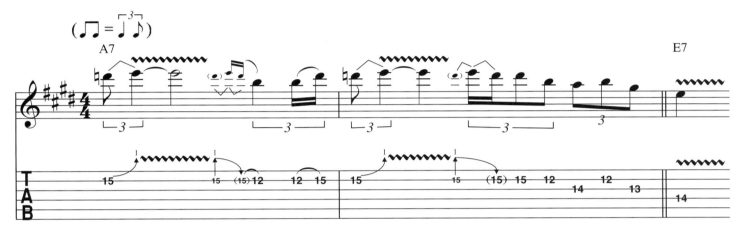

The next two short phrases feature the two most common unison bends. In the first, the G string is bent up a whole step at the 14th fret with the 3rd finger (A to B) to match the B played by the 1st finger on the B string. After the bend, flatten your 1st finger into a barre to grab the double stop on the top two strings.

Unison Bend 1 from "Hide Away" *(Eric Clapton)*

TRACK 37

In the following phrase, the ♭7th of the pentatonic scale (D on the B string's 15th fret) is bent up a whole step to match the tonic (E on the high E string's 12th fret). As usual, your 3rd finger performs the bends. This is the same unison bend we learned earlier in the excerpt from "Steppin' Out," only this time we are in the key of E rather than G. In a minor pentatonic scale, raising the ♭7th to match the tonic and the 4th to match the 5th are by far the most common and popular bending moves.

Unison Bend 2 from "Hide Away" *(Eric Clapton)*

TRACK 38

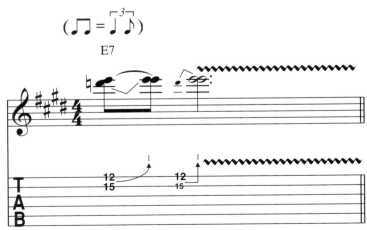

Our final Clapton example (for now) includes multiple double stop bends played by barring the G and B strings with your 1st and 3rd fingers (for the 12th and 14th fret bends, respectively). These can be a bit tough, as it's harder to bend strings with a flattened finger than an arched one; you're also bending two strings at once (obviously), so additional strength is needed to push them the required distance. Each of the bends here are up a half step (except the final quarter-step bend), so you don't have to raise the strings too far; the main concern (in any double-stop bend, really) is that the higher note reach its destination. If you hit that target, the lower string should get there too. So, in this phrase, your main goal is raising the C♯ to D on the B string. An exception occurs on the final beat of the lick when the G is raised to G♯ during the 12th fret bend; focus on raising the G string by pushing a little harder from the tip of your 1st finger. The B string will follow, and you should be able to get the desired quarter step lift for the final note.

Double-Stop Bends from "Hide Away" *(Eric Clapton)*

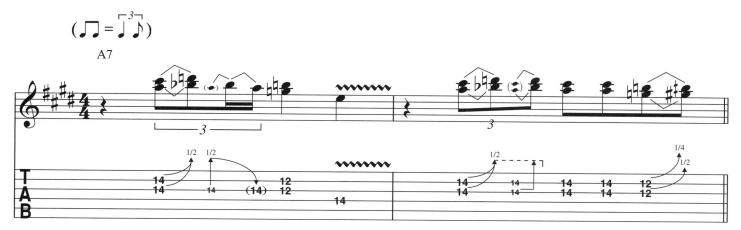

In the following lick from "Texas Flood," Stevie Ray Vaughan bends the high E string a total of 12 times in a wide variety of ways and distances. Be sure you know how all your target notes should sound before you get started. Also note the various bending techniques at play here: the initial bend is struck and raised simultaneously (lifting C to D); the second bend is a pre-bend (same bend but the string is raised before it is struck); the third bend is a pre-bend followed by a release back down to its unbent position; and the fourth bend (A♯ to B) is in time and in a specific rhythm (namely, on the 10th and 11th beats of the opening measure). In measure 2 and the tail end of the phrase (after the double bar), we bend up a half step and push the string farther (first up three quarter steps above B—somewhere between C and C♯—and then up a whole step, raising C to C♯ and finally D). Wow, that's a lot of bending and a lot of detail!

Play this one strictly in 6th position so that your 3rd finger performs the 8th fret bends, your 2nd finger bends on the 7th fret, and your 1st finger plays the 6th fret bends. This is an easy one to gloss over and merely approximate, but do your best to play it right, in the correct rhythm, in tune, and employing all of the different techniques Vaughan has on display. No one said this was going to be easy!

Combination Bending Phrase from "Texas Flood" *(Stevie Ray Vaughan)*

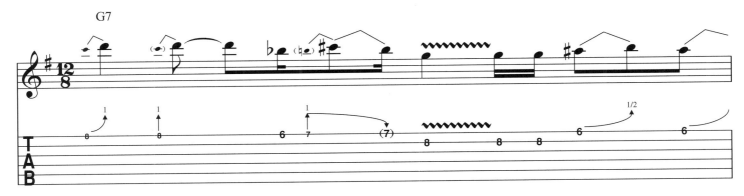

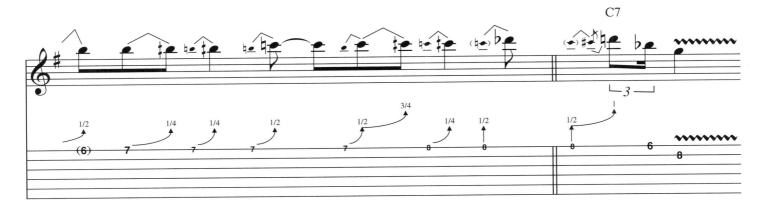

The final three examples in this chapter bring us back to Albert King for some highly demanding techniques. Albert's dropped tuning lowered the string tension considerably—but the lower tension shouldn't gloss over the fact that Albert (much like B.B. King and Stevie Ray) had tremendously strong hands though. In fact, he used tremendously heavy gauged strings, which somewhat countered the lighter tension he would normally achieve from detuning. You may never develop the strength of these players, who likely had some innate gifts as well as years of playing under their belts, but you can certainly try your best and get the most out of what you have to work with!

The lick below begins with a pre-bend from C to D on the high E string. As soon as you hit the string, push it up another whole step, all the way to E (a full major 3rd above C). Play the D and E notes you're targeting before you try the phrase, use your 3rd finger to bend and your 1st and 2nd fingers to assist, and push, push, push that string. Just don't snap it.

Overbend Lick from "Crosscut Saw" (Albert King)

A7

In the following excerpt from "Laundromat Blues," King performs the same overbending technique (pushing the minor 3rd of a pentatonic scale up a whole-step and then a full major 3rd, all the way to the 4th of the scale). The key is B♭ rather than A, but the technique is very much the same. Listen to your bending targets (E♭ and F), particularly if you're trying this one right after the previous example, because of the different key. Also note that the initial overbend is not returned to its unbent position but rather a half-step above it (D rather than D♭).

Overbend Lick from "Laundromat Blues" (Albert King)

B♭7

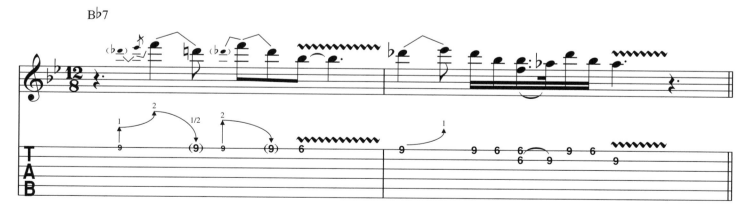

Finally, let's take a look at this longer excerpt covering the first five measures of a 12 bar blues in B♭. If you thought the previous examples were tough, wait till you get a load of this one: the same overbending techniques are at work here but are now applied to double stop bends, so you have to push the B and high E strings up a whole step, then all the way to a major 3rd above the starting position, with a 3rd finger barre. Note that some of these are pre-bends, others are played in time, and still others are released gradually. The overall effect is wild, savage, and captures the anger expressed in the lyrics ("You've been meetin' your man babe, down at the local Laundromat"). The menacing bends reflect their chilling threat ("I don't want you to get so clean baby, you just might wash your life away").

By all means work to get a handle on these exceedingly difficult techniques. But don't brush off the bigger picture: the blues is about storytelling, attitude, and emotion as much (if not more) than it's about chops and overall technical prowess.

Overbending Double Stops from "Laundromat Blues" *(Albert King)*

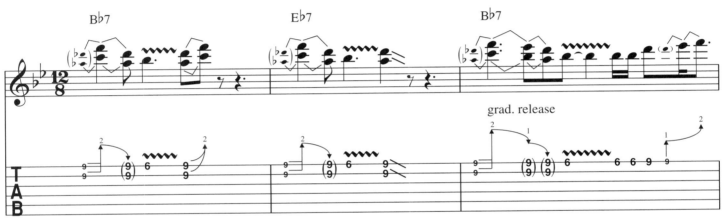

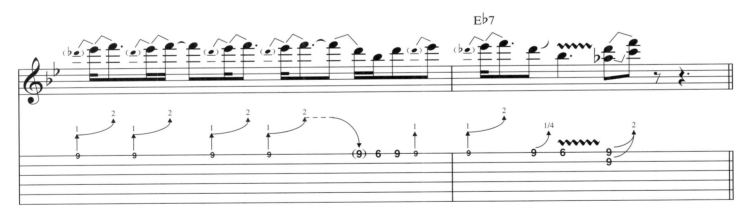

CHAPTER 5

Double Stops

In the previous chapter, we examined a handful of examples in which double stops were used in bends; in this chapter, we'll look at a few of the many other ways in which they can be employed in solos. Note that these are merely the tip of the iceberg and that the subject could easily fill an entire book and still not be exhaustive. Because of the very nature of the guitar, double stop combinations are nearly infinite; any two strings can be employed, and the intervallic distances between them can be as near or as far as one can imagine (and/or reach).

That being said, let's take a look at some examples that use double stops in ways that are common to the collective blues vocabulary. In our first example, Joe Bonamassa plays a simple repeated phrase in the C minor pentatonic scale and uses a 1st finger barre to play the double stops on the G and B strings. 1st and 3rd finger double stop barre combinations work particularly well in this scale.

Double-Stop Lick from "Left Overs" *(Joe Bonamassa)*

In the opening phrase from "Laundromat Blues" below, Albert King plays from the B♭ major pentatonic scale, adding vibrato to a major 3rd/5th combination on the G and B strings. Use your 1st finger for the higher note and your 2nd finger on the G string. Throughout this song, major and minor pentatonic ideas are combined frequently, giving the song a level of sophistication that might otherwise be lacking with only one or the other.

Major Pentatonic Double Stop Lick from "Laundromat Blues" *(Albert King)*

Words and Music by Sandy Jones, Jr.
Copyright © 1966 IRVING MUSIC, INC.
Copyright Renewed
All Rights Reserved   Used by Permission

In the following excerpt from "Come When I Call," John Mayer uses the same note combination (D and F), but plays them over a G7 chord, rather than the B♭7 chord in the previous example. In the new key, these notes represent the 5th and ♭7th, respectively. Slide into the double stop with your 1st and 2nd fingers, strike it repeatedly, then finish out the phrase by dropping down into 3rd position on beat 4.

Sliding Double Stop Lick from "Come When I Call" *(John Mayer)*

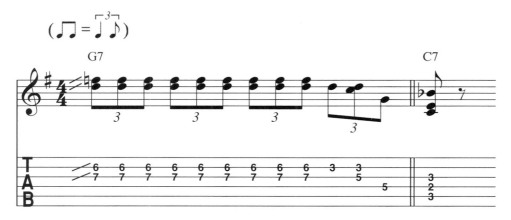

Words and Music by John Mayer
Copyright (©) 2005 Sony/ATV Music Publishing LLC and Specific Harm Music
All Rights Administered by Sony/ATV Music Publishing LLC, 8 Music Square West, Nashville, TN 37203
International Copyright Secured   All Rights Reserved

The next three examples are from "Blues Intro" in the key of C. In the first, Mayer uses the same combination (the 5th and ♭7th) of the minor pentatonic scale as well as the same fingering. The diagonal slashes in both the tablature and standard notation indicate that these double stops are to be *tremolo picked*, meaning alternate-picked as fast as possible. The durations of the notes are as indicated, but during each indicated rhythm, you should pick the heck out of them. In the second measure, flatten your 1st finger to include the E♭ on the high E string's 11th fret, turning the double stop into a "triple stop," before ending the lick with some pentatonic eighth notes.

Tremolo-Picked Double Stops from "Blues Intro" *(John Mayer)*

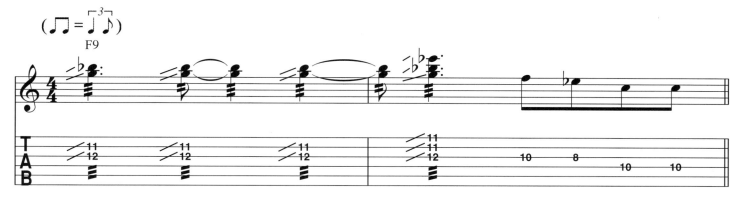

In the next lick, Mayer barres the D and G strings at the 8th fret with his 1st finger (playing the ♭7th and minor 3rd of the C7 chord) and uses his 3rd finger to hammer on to the 10th fret of the D string. In measure 2, he pulls off from his 3rd finger to his 1st finger, then slides down to the E♭ on the A string's 6th fret, picking only once for all three notes.

Hammer-on Double Stops from "Blues Intro" *(John Mayer)*

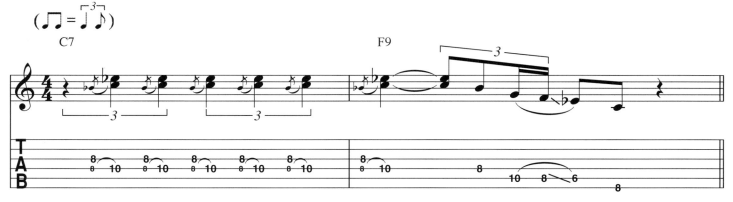

The jazzy excerpt below should be played entirely in 8th position, save the final note, which should be played by simply shifting your 1st finger down a fret. Begin by sliding into the initial C note with your 3rd finger and play the 8th and 10th fret double stops with 1st and 3rd finger barres, respectively. In each measure, the G string hammer-on from E♭ to E should be played by the 2nd finger. The combination of major and minor 3rds over the C7 chord is classic blues vocabulary.

Jazzy Double Stops from "Blues Intro" *(John Mayer)*

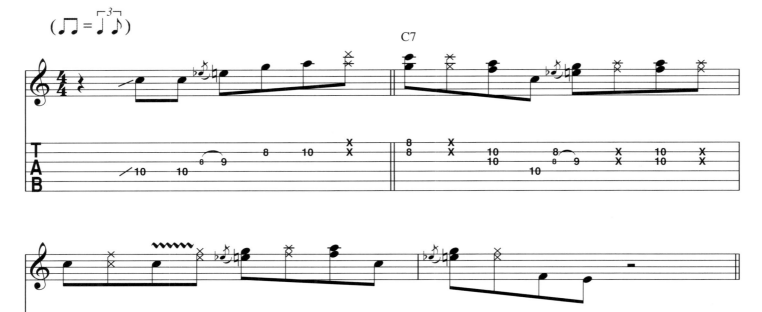

The next example is by Eric Clapton and instead of combining 3rds and 4ths, the interval between all notes is a 6th. The notes are also spread between the G and high E strings, rather than between two consecutive strings. This can sometimes present a problem in terms of picking, but throughout this lick the notes on the G string are to be played by the 2nd finger, which can be flattened slightly to mute the open B string from ringing. The 3rd finger should play all the high E string notes. This allows you to pick normally, except in the case of the open G and high E strings. One solution is to use a Nashville style hybrid picking approach, in which the G string is picked and the high E string is plucked with the middle finger of the right hand. Parallel 6ths are a familiar sound in both blues and country guitar.

Sliding 6ths from "Hide Away" *(Eric Clapton)*

Let's finish up by looking at three classic double stop licks from Stevie Ray Vaughan's "Texas Flood." The first features the same repeated, 1st finger barring move with the 2nd finger hammering on to the G string a fret above that we observed in earlier examples. However, this time the C♯, D, and F represent the ♭5th, perfect 5th, and ♭7th in relation to the G7 chord (rather than the minor 3rd, major 3rd, and 5th). This is an easy phrase to play but one that demonstrates the power of simple, rhythmic repetition very well.

Repeated Double Stops from "Texas Flood" *(Stevie Ray Vaughan)*

The slick, driving phrase below begins with a hammer-on from the 1st to the 3rd finger and a subsequent slide up to the 7th fret on the G string. The 2nd finger then plays all the F notes (on the B string's 6th fret) with the 3rd finger taking the lower note of the double stops. At the end of the lick, we slide back down to the 3rd position G minor pentatonic "box."

Sliding Double Stops from "Texas Flood" (*Stevie Ray Vaughan*)

The lick that follows combines numerous techniques in one brief, very hip phrase played over measures 4 and 5 of the blues form (the I chord, G7, moving to the IV, C7). Begin with a 3rd finger half step bend on the G string, then play the first double stop with your 2nd and 3rd fingers and bend the notes up slightly a quarter step. This tritone grouping represents the 6th (E) and minor 3rd (B♭) relative to a G7 chord, a somewhat pungent and dissonant sound. The very Hendrix-esque D string trill later in the opening measure should be played by hammering on and pulling off rapidly between your 1st and 3rd fingers. Play the barred double stops in measure 2 with your 1st finger taking the 3rd fret notes and your 3rd finger sliding up from the 4th to the 5th fret.

Double Stops and Trill from "Texas Flood" (*Stevie Ray Vaughan*)

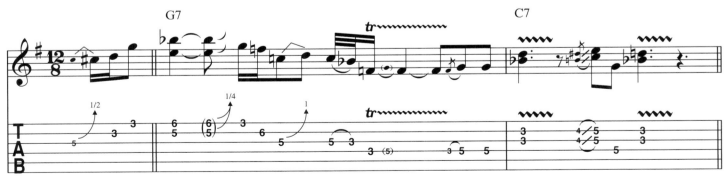

CHAPTER 6

Turnarounds

The final two measures of the 12-bar blues form are perhaps the most crucial, affording the creative player a chance to put their individual stamp on a solo in a wide variety of ways. The *turnaround* is also a repository of classic blues vocabulary, some of which we will unearth in the examples to follow. While the subject is complex enough to serve as the focus of an entire book (and it has; Cherry Lane's *75 Blues Turnarounds*, by Michael DoCampo, with Toby Wine, is an excellent resource), we can skim the surface with a brief theoretical discussion and some choice licks by the masters themselves. First and foremost, it is essential to understand exactly what is going on harmonically during the turnaround. In the most basic, pared-down blues progressions, the rhythm section either sits on the I chord during the final two measures of the form or plays the I chord in bar 11 and the V chord in bar 12. This obviously requires no explanation; the soloist may choose to acknowledge the end of the form or not as the mood strikes them. However, there are other progressions commonly employed during the turnaround, the most common of which is shown below in the key of A:

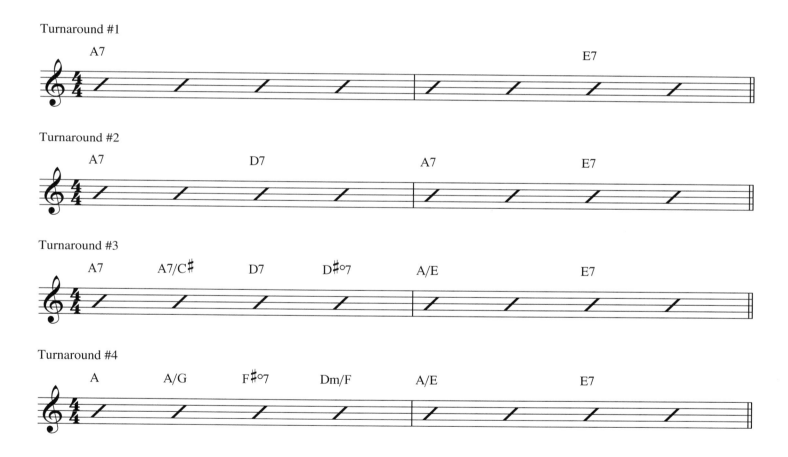

The first is quite simple and merely shifts from the I chord to the V chord during the latter half of the final measure. Often the soloist will play a phrase that descends in some way to the 5th of the pentatonic scale. The second turnaround introduces a bit more root movement by climbing to the IV chord and back again before hitting the V. The third variation also lands on the IV chord during beat 3 of the first measure but gets there in an interesting way. A rising bass line moves chromatically from the major 3rd (C♯) to the 5th (E), hitting various inversions along the way (A7 with the 3rd, C♯, and the 5th, E, in the bass). The D♯°7 diminished chord serves as a chromatic connector between D7 and A/E. In the fourth variation, the bass moves down chromatically from the ♭7th (G) to the 5th. This time, the inversions include A/G, F♯°7 (same as A°7), D minor with its 3rd in the bass (F), and the tonic chord, A, with its 5th in the bass (E). These progressions are often glossed over by guitarists but will be implied by the bassist and often stated explicitly by a keyboardist, as they're somewhat easier to play on that instrument. That being said, one should absolutely learn to play the chords to these chromatic turnarounds in a variety of keys and positions; they're fun and challenging and may open your eyes to a host of soloing and accompaniment possibilities.

Let's start by looking at two Albert King licks from "Crosscut Saw." The band merely implies the E7 chord in this song, but in each example King is sure to make his lines descend to an E to emphasize the end of the form. Begin the first lick on your 1st finger, slide down to 3rd position, then shift down farther at the end of the opening measure to play the C on the B string with your 1st finger.

Turnaround Lick 1 from "Crosscut Saw" (Albert King)

Later in the same song, King plays a similar turnaround lick. While both are straightforward minor pentatonic phrases, this one is a little easier in terms of fingering, as you remain in 3rd position until reaching down with your 1st finger to grab the 2nd fret notes that end the line.

Turnaround Lick 2 from "Crosscut Saw" *(Albert King)*

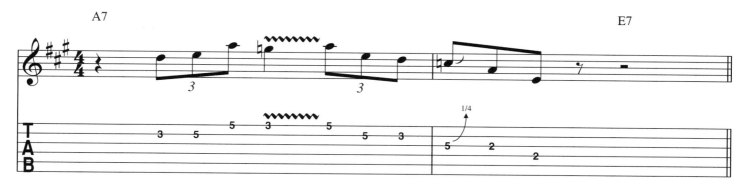

Words and Music by R.G. Ford
Copyright © 1969 IRVING MUSIC, INC.
Copyright Renewed
All Rights Reserved   Used by Permission

While we're on the subject of Albert King, let's move up a half step and take a peek at a turnaround lick from "Laundromat Blues," in which the V chord (F7) is given a full measure at the end of each chorus. Start this one by sliding up the B string with your 3rd finger and play the half step bend with your 1st finger. You'll need to downshift twice to finish out the lick—first by reaching down to grab the final note of measure 1 with your 1st finger, then dropping down into 1st position in measure 2 to play the E♭ on the D string with your 1st finger as well. This is still basically a straightforward pentatonic phrase, but the position shifting, bend, and use of the "blue note" (the ♭5th, E) give this one a little added sophistication and make it an obvious candidate for addition to any blues guitarist's repertoire of licks. Transposing it to a variety of keys will aid in memorization (and usefulness).

Turnaround Lick from "Laundromat Blues" *(Albert King)*

Words and Music by Sandy Jones, Jr.
Copyright © 1966 IRVING MUSIC, INC.
Copyright Renewed
All Rights Reserved   Used by Permission

Talk about classic vocabulary: this turnaround from Clapton's "Hide Away" solo in E fits the description to a T and belongs in any blues soloist's bag of tricks. Stay in 12th position for the duration and reach out with your 3rd finger to grab the 15th fret D on the B string. The juxtaposition of minor and major 3rds (G and G♯, respectively) figures prominently here. You'll definitely want to learn this one in as many keys as possible.

Turnaround Lick from "Hide Away" *(Eric Clapton)*

TRACK 57

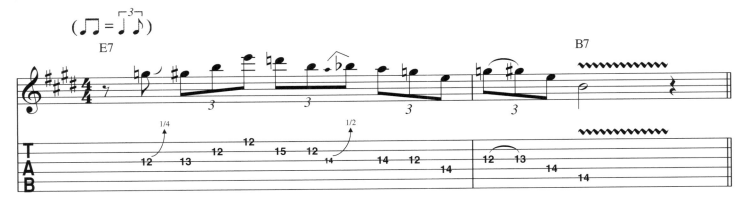

By Freddie King and Sonny Thompson
Copyright © 1961 by Fort Knox Music Inc. and Bug Music-Trio Music Company
Copyright Renewed
International Copyright Secured   All Rights Reserved
Used by Permission

The following lick from B.B. King's "Five Long Years" is played over the stationary I chord (C), but King still emphasizes the end of the 12-bar form by descending to the 5th. This is a deceptively sophisticated phrase that's quite intricate rhythmically, so take the time to learn exactly where in each measure the notes should fall. The line begins in 11th position, with the 3rd finger playing the 13th fret bend-and-release and pulling off to the 1st finger. Follow up by sliding into 8th position at the end of measure 1 and the start of measure 2. Notice that the first descending sequence outlines a C major triad (C–G–E–C) and is immediately followed by a C minor triad (G–E♭–C–G).

Turnaround Lick from "Five Long Years" *(B.B. King)*

TRACK 58

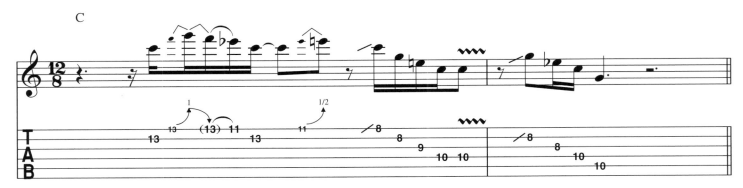

Words and Music by B.B. King
Copyright © 1966 by Universal Music - Careers
Copyright Renewed
International Copyright Secured   All Rights Reserved

Let's take a look at three turnaround phrases by Joe Bonamassa in the key of C. The first and easiest of the three is an uptempo lick from "Left Overs" that begins with a double stop, hammer-on combination in which the 2nd finger plays the Bb on the B string while the 3rd finger performs the hammer-on below. Follow up by sliding down the G string into 8th position, then finish out the line by sliding up the A string to the 15th fret and down the low E string. This is another straightforward turnaround lick worth learning in a number of different keys to have at your disposal whenever you want to pull it out.

Turnaround Lick from "Left Overs" *(Joe Bonamassa)*

The following two examples are from Bonamassa's slow, smoldering rendition of "Blues Deluxe." Note the I–IV–I–V turnaround progression employed. These are a bit harder, so take your time working them up to speed. The lick below stays in the 8th position pentatonic "box" but adds a hammer-on to the major 3rd (E) in the opening measure; the A string slide in measure 2 should be played with the 2nd finger. As usual, the G string bend-and-release is taken by the 3rd finger. A truly classic phrase.

Turnaround Lick 1 from "Blues Deluxe" *(Joe Bonamassa)*

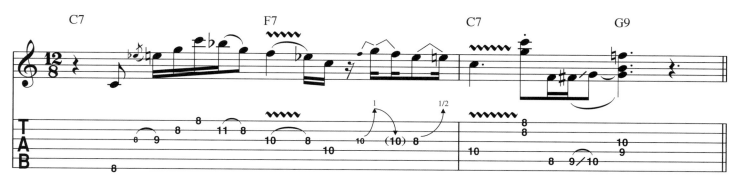

The next lick is harder still, although it also sticks very closely to 8th position pentatonic "box" playing. It's simply faster and more ornate, with multiple bends and trickier rhythms. The only shifting you'll need to do is a quick 3rd finger slide up the G string from the 10th to the 11th fret near the end of measure 1. The rootless G9 chord should be played with the 1st finger on the D string and the 3rd finger barring the G and B strings. All the bends should be played by the 3rd finger as is par for the course.

Turnaround Lick 2 from "Blues Deluxe" *(Joe Bonamassa)*

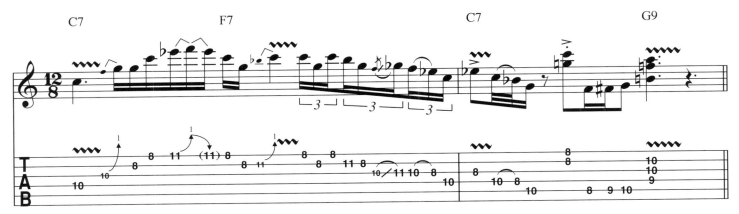

Let's turn our attention back to Stevie Ray Vaughan, starting with two turnarounds from "Pride and Joy," a shuffle blues in E that allows for extensive use of open strings. Because of this, these licks are much harder to transpose to other keys, but they were simply too cool to omit from these pages. In the first, slide into the repeated double stops with your 1st and 2nd fingers, then slide down the G string with your 2nd finger. The lick ends by climbing up the blues scale (the minor pentatonic with the ♭5th added) from the open low E string to the B on the A string's 2nd fret.

Turnaround Lick 1 from "Pride and Joy" *(Stevie Ray Vaughan)*

The following lick is very similar to the previous one and ends in exactly the same way but also introduces some subtle variations—namely the downwards rake across the top three strings and the subsequent 2nd finger slide and pull-off on the G string. While the strategic use of open strings is a big part of the appeal of these licks, they can be replicated in other keys. It's a bit of a challenge, but your 1st finger can play all the open string notes in another key with a little forethought and practice. Give it a shot.

Turnaround Lick 2 from "Pride and Joy" *(Stevie Ray Vaughan)*

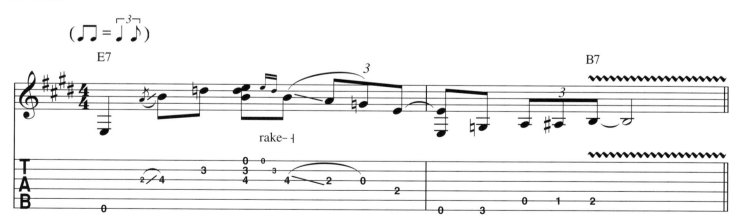

The last three turnarounds are each taken from "Texas Flood" and are played over the ascending chromatic bass line progression discussed earlier (G–G7/B–C–C#°7–G–D7). They're pretty tough, so take your time getting them together, paying particular attention to the little details and the very specific rhythms in each. The first lick sticks to the 3rd position G minor pentatonic scale for the duration, augmenting it with both the 9th (A) and ♭9th (A♭) relative to the G chord in the first measure. Unlike many previous examples, it's a good idea to use your 4th finger for all of the 6th fret notes here, as the speed of the line and the many 3rd finger bends make this the most advantageous fingering.

Turnaround Lick 1 from "Texas Flood" *(Stevie Ray Vaughan)*

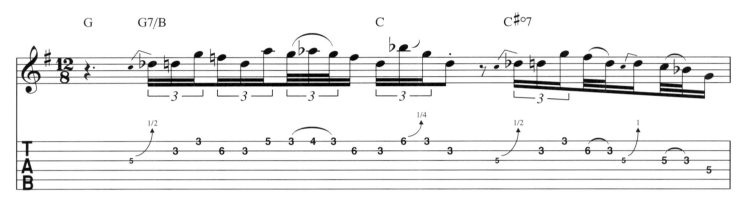

The next lick begins with a descent through the G blues scale, followed by a quick D string trill between the 1st and 3rd fingers. Vaughan then returns to the idea shown in the previous example, including both 9th and ♭9th degrees in the line. The two 6th fret bends on the high E string should, however, be played by the 3rd finger, unless your 4th finger is exceptionally strong and agile.

Turnaround Lick 2 from "Texas Flood" *(Stevie Ray Vaughan)*

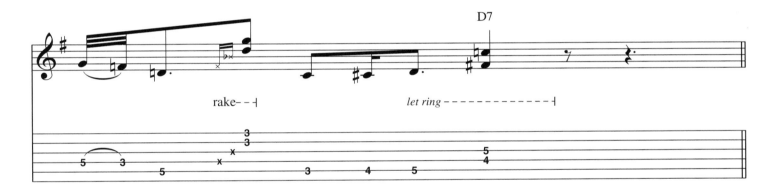

Our final turnaround lick is also the final turnaround of the song and begins with lightly bent double stops played by the 2nd and 3rd fingers on the B and high E strings, respectively. Reach out to play the barred 6th and 5th fret double stops that follow with your 3rd and 2nd fingers. To play the "inside" notes of the A♭ chord, use your 3rd finger on the B string and your 2nd finger on the D string, flattening it slightly to prevent the unused open G string from ringing. Use the same technique for the final G7 chords, adding your 1st finger to the A string's 2nd fret to get to the low B and your 4th finger to play the G on the high E string. This is a great song ending phrase worth learning in multiple keys.

Ending Turnaround Lick from "Texas Flood" *(Stevie Ray Vaughan)*

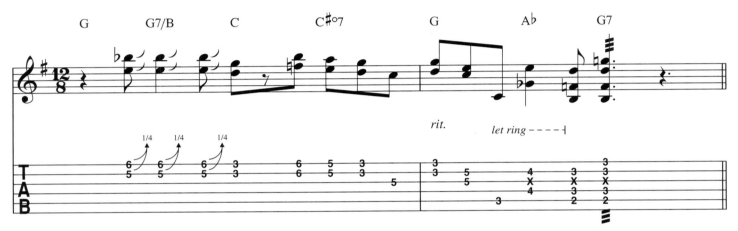

CHAPTER 7

Classic Licks

The title of this chapter says it all: these are classic, must-know licks and phrases that are likely to find an indispensable place in your soloing repertoire. They're grouped by the artist and then by level of difficulty. Let's get started with some great B.B. King licks from "Five Long Years," in the key of C. The first short phrase begins with a 3rd finger bend and release. The lick ends with a pull-off from the 3rd to the 2nd finger, which then slides down the B string to the 8th fret. Note the use of the B rather than the Bᵇ here; this lick is played over the final measure of the blues form and, while the band doesn't explicitly play the V chord (G7), B.B. implies it with this note, which represents the major 3rd of that chord.

Bend and Release Lick from "Five Long Years" *(B.B. King)*

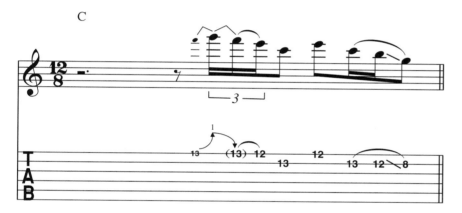

The lick below is very similar but begins with a standard whole step bend rather than a bend and release. The B string pull-off and slide is now from the 3rd to the 1st finger, and the B♭ rather than the B is employed, sticking strictly to notes from the C minor pentatonic scale.

Bend, Pull-off, and Slide Lick from "Five Long Years" *(B.B. King)*

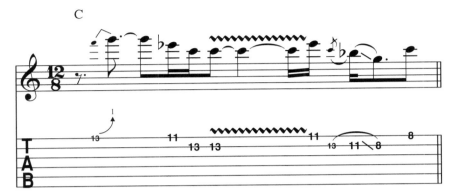

Our third lick from this song starts the same way as the previous phrase: with a whole step bend on the high E string's 13th fret. Near the end of the opening measure, we drop down to 8th position and descend through the notes of a C major triad and back up again. The lick ends with a classic move, hitting the same note, the tonic (C), on two different strings (the high E and the B string), playing up the subtle textural differences between them.

Position Shifting Phrase from "Five Long Years" *(B.B. King)*

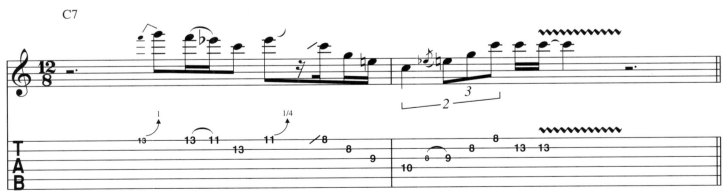

Let's change gears and look at three licks from "Lucille," B.B.'s sprawling tribute to his beloved Gibson ES-335 in the key of E. The first is just about as classic as they come; a 3rd finger G string bend pushes A up to B, matching the 12th fret, B string note that follows. At the end of the lick, a 15th fret bend on the B string pushes D to E. These are the most common bending moves in the minor pentatonic scale by a long margin.

G and B String Bends from "Lucille" *(B.B. King)*

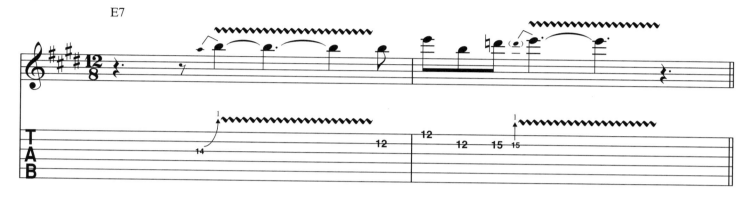

The next lick is played over the turnaround but works pretty much anywhere within the blues form. Stay in 12th position but play each of the three bends with your 3rd finger. Notice how B.B. outlines an A7 chord with the G–A–C#–E sequence at the end of the first measure. He's implying the I–IV–I–V turnaround even if the rhythm section is not!

Turnaround Lick from "Lucille" *(B.B. King)*

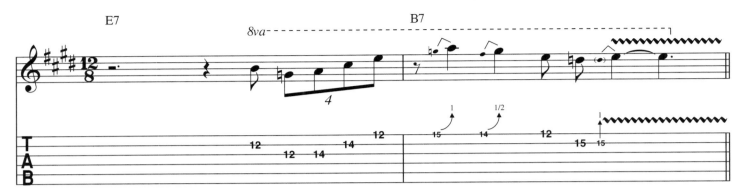

The tasty phrase below demonstrates how, even if he is very much centered on the minor pentatonic scale, B.B. still acknowledges the changing chords by playing the major 3rd of the A7 chord (C#) in the first measure and the major 3rd of the E7 chord (G#) in the second. Use your 1st finger for all of the 11th and 12th fret notes and your 3rd finger for the slide into the 15th fret B♭. The position shifts in this lick are subtle and smooth.

IV–I Lick with Major 3rds from "Lucille" *(B.B. King)*

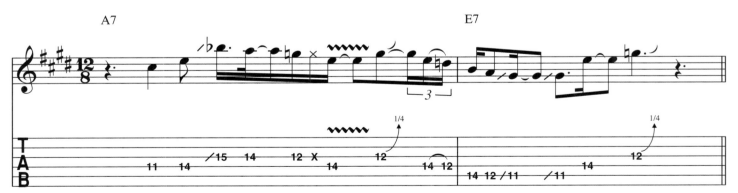

Now let's check out some John Mayer licks that make it clear just how well-versed he is in traditional blues vocabulary. Being a mega-pop star has its stigmas in the blues world, but anyone denying Mayer's skill and knowledge of the genre is simply kidding themselves at this point. Check out the opening phrase from "Come When I Call"; it's melodic, swinging, and totally authentic. After beginning the excerpt with a 3rd finger, grace note hammer-on, drop down into 3rd position for much of the remainder of the lick. Dig the way he peppers the line with chords and double stops, providing his own accompaniment.

Intro Lick from "Come When I Call" *(John Mayer)*

The next phrase has two particularly interesting facets: the juxtaposition of 16th note and triplet rhythms, and the combination of G major and minor pentatonic scale tones. In a shuffle blues, players can get trapped into excessively triplet-heavy phrasing because these rhythms fit so well into the overall groove, but they can become tiresome and dull without variation. By working 16th notes into this lick, Mayer busts out of the predictable triplet rut in style. The line gets added sophistication with the inclusion of the major 6th (E), major 3rd (B), and ♭5th (D♭) as well.

16th note and Triplet Combination Phrase from "Come When I Call" *(John Mayer)*

Let's move onto Mayer's uptempo "Blues Intro" in C, beginning with his swinging opening phrase. Minor pentatonic notes are embellished with the major 9th (D) and 3rd (E) during the final 2nd finger hammer-on on the G string.

Intro Lick from "Blues Intro" *(John Mayer)*

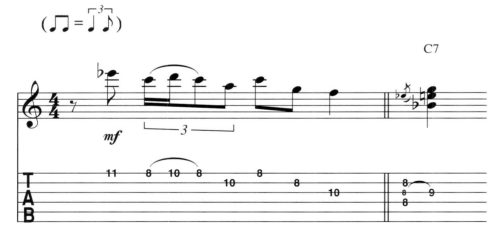

The lick below begins by hitting the C on the B string's 13th fret, then jumps up an octave to grab the super-high C notes on the 20th fret of the high E string. End the phrase by dropping into 8th position as you close out the line.

Octave-Jumping Lick from "Blues Intro" *(John Mayer)*

TRACK 76

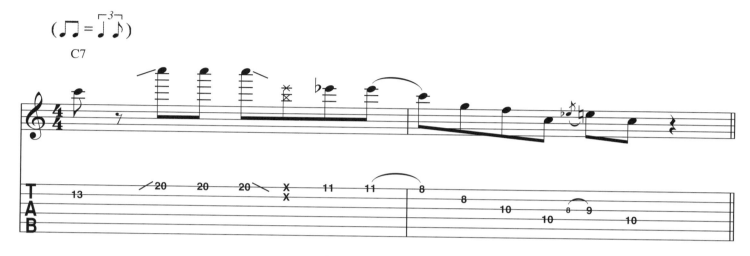

Our final John Mayer lick is a straight-ahead bit of classic blues vocabulary featuring a 3rd finger G string "pitch-matching" bend that raises F to G before we hit the same note on the B string's 8th fret. The downwards slide and pull-off later in the opening measure should be initiated by the 3rd finger as well.

Bend and Slide Lick from "Blues Intro" *(John Mayer)*

TRACK 77

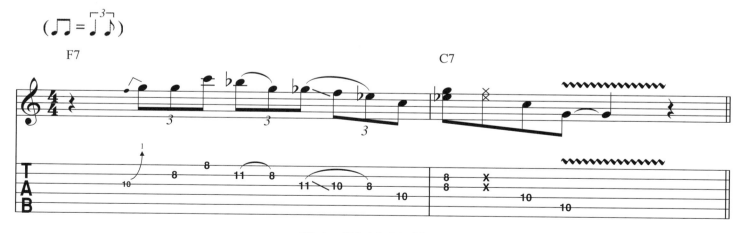

Let's move on to Eric Clapton and check out a handful of great licks and phrases from the master's early work with John Mayall. The eight-bar riff below begins his famous rendition of "Steppin' Out" and is played entirely in 3rd position using notes from the G and D minor pentatonic scales. It's easy and fun to play and totally iconic to boot.

Intro Riff from "Steppin' Out" *(Eric Clapton)*

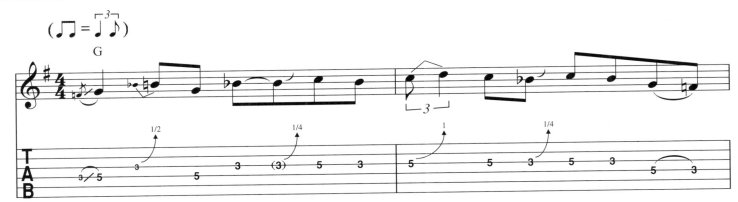

Words and Music by James Bracken
Copyright © 1959 (Renewed) by Conrad Music (BMI)
All Rights Administered by BMG Chrysalis
International Copyright Secured   All Rights Reserved
Used by Permission

The lick below contains some familiar bending moves and a few subtle details that make it a little harder than it looks. The initial 3rd finger bend on the G string pushes C up to C♯ then a half step farther to D on a single pick-stroke. Be sure that each of the targeted pitches is heard clearly. In the second half of the measure, the same note is pre-bent a whole step and then pulled off to the 1st finger, which bends the B♭ at the G string's 3rd fret up a quarter step.

Combination Bending Phrase from "Steppin Out" *(Eric Clapton)*

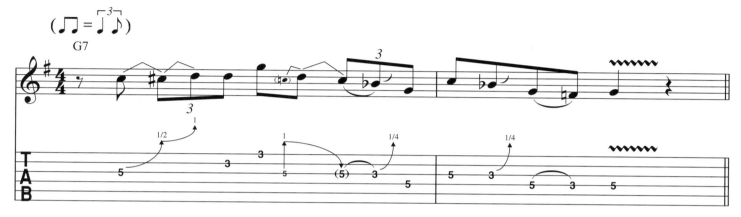

The following Clapton licks are all from "Hide Away," a medium shuffle blues in E. The first mixes major and minor pentatonic scales neatly, with the major 3rd (G♯) and 9th (F♯) supplementing the more common minor tones. This one stays strictly in 12th position, with the 3rd finger doing all the bending work.

Major and Minor Pentatonic Combo Lick from "Hide Away" *(Eric Clapton)*

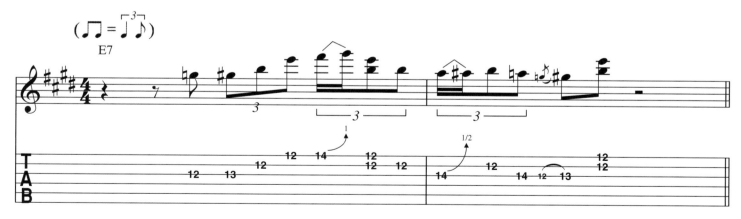

Here's Clapton's take on a very familiar minor pentatonic bending lick that's textbook blues guitar. The 3rd finger plays the first two bends (including a bend, release, and pull-off on beat 3), while the 1st finger ends the phrase by bending the G up a half step to the major 3rd (G♯).

Classic Bending Lick from "Hide Away" *(Eric Clapton)*

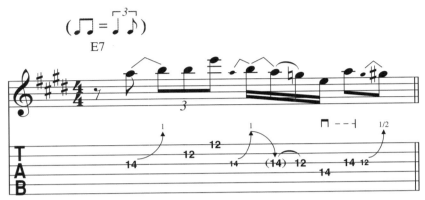

Here's a slick lick that combines a number of bending techniques. Stay in 12th position and use your 3rd finger for each bend except the 12th fret G string bend. Extend your 3rd finger a bit for the 15th fret bends on the high E string the way Clapton does it. The first three bends are in time and rhythmically specific, while the final one is a pre-bend-and-release, followed by a pull-off to the 1st finger.

Combination Bending Lick 1 from "Hide Away" *(Eric Clapton)*

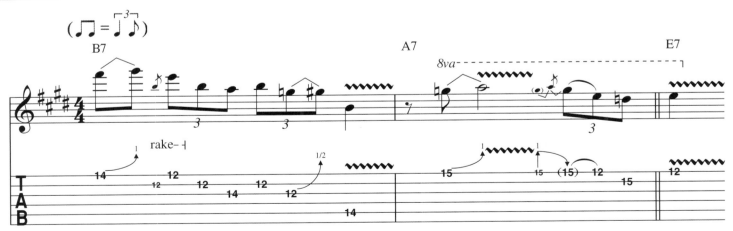

The following lick begins with a 3rd finger double stop bend on the B and high E strings. Bend the high E string up and catch the B string under your fingertip in the process, being sure to raise the higher pitch a full whole step up from G to A (the lower note should follow suit). The rest of the lick sticks closely to the 12th position E minor pentatonic blues "box," with the addition of the major 3rd (G♯) in the 12th fret G string bend in measure 2 and the barred 14th fret double stops that include the major 6th (C♯). Although Clapton plays this one over the V–IV progression in measures 9 and 10 of the blues form, it works equally well over stationary E7 or A7 chords.

Combination Bending Lick 2 from "Hide Away" *(Eric Clapton)*

TRACK 83

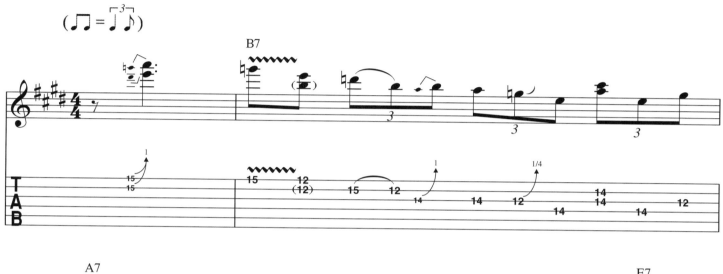

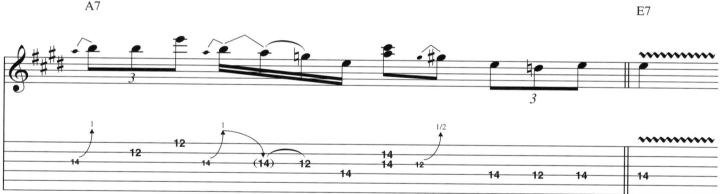

The following lick from Joe Bonamassa's uptempo C blues "Left Overs" is played over the last four measures of the 12-bar form and contains some subtle position shifting maneuvers. In the first measure, play the hammer-on/pull-off/slide combination with your 1st and 3rd fingers, sliding down the G string with your 1st finger into 8th position. At the end of the measure, slide back up to the 12th fret with your 3rd finger, then downshift on beat 3 of the second measure so that your 3rd finger plays the 10th fret F. Like the previous example, this one also works equally well over a stationary chord (C7).

Position Shifting Lick from "Left Overs" *(Joe Bonamassa)*

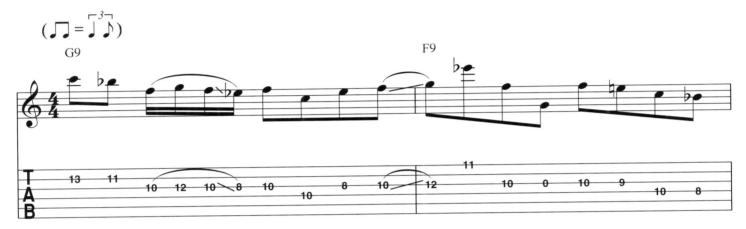

The next three licks are taken from Bonamassa's smoldering rendition of "Blues Deluxe" and are a quite a step up in terms of difficulty, so take your time getting them under your fingers. The following phrase is made up of C minor pentatonic scale notes and bends in 8th position, but it's super-quick and rhythmically intricate. The only shifting you'll need to do is for the initial E♭–F–E♭ note combo and subsequent bend; play these notes with your 2nd and 3rd fingers, bending with your 2nd finger, then return to 8th position for the duration of the lick. All of the remaining 11th fret notes should be played with the 3rd finger. This is an intense burst of blues shredding but still needs to be rhythmically precise and "in the pocket," so don't try it at full speed until you're ready and know exactly where in the measure each note needs to fall.

Minor Pentatonic Lick from "Blues Deluxe" *(Joe Bonamassa)*

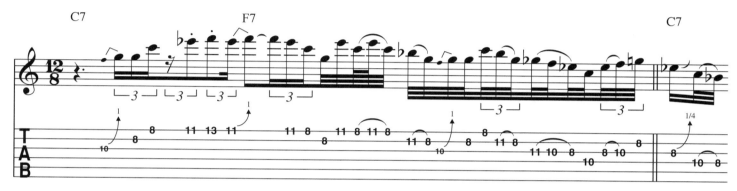

Here's a great lick Joe plays over the IV chord (F7) that is fairly easily transposed to fit any dominant chord—simply shift the entire phrase up or down the requisite number of frets so that it begins on the root of any chord over which you want to apply it. Begin with your 1st finger and reach out to grab the major 3rd of the chord with your 4th finger. Stay in 8th position throughout the lick and play the 11th fret notes (and bend) with your 3rd finger.

IV Chord Lick from "Blues Deluxe" *(Joe Bonamassa)*

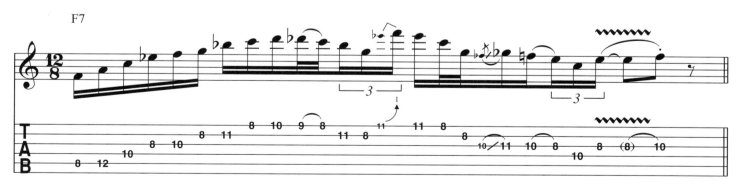

Here's another fast and intricate lick that demands a bit more attention in terms of fingering in addition to the sheer chops necessary to pull it off. Play the initial 10th fret bend with your 3rd finger and use your 4th finger to grab the 10th fret D above, then quickly shift to play the 10th fret high E string bends with your 3rd finger. Stay in 8th position, with your 3rd finger extended to play all 11th frets in the first measure until the final B♭, which should be played with the 4th finger. This will allow you to bend the G string with your 3rd finger immediately after. Shift up again to play the final bend in the measure with your 3rd finger and grab the C that follows with your 4th finger. After bending the G string once more, play the remaining notes on that string in the following extended 8th position fingering: 1st and 2nd fingers taking the 8th and 10th fret notes, respectively, with your 3rd finger playing the 11th and 12th fret notes. At the end of the phrase, slide into the 14th fret A with your 2nd finger and play the C notes on the B string's 13th fret with your 1st finger.

Position Shifting Lick from "Blues Deluxe" *(Joe Bonamassa)*

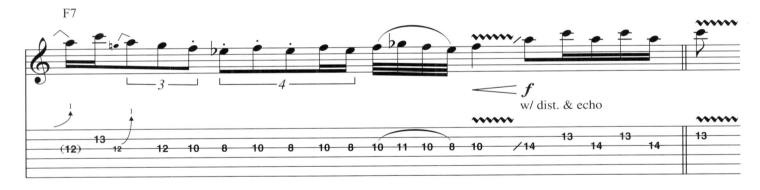

Words and Music by Rod Stewart and Jeff Beck
© 1968 (Renewed 1996) ROD STEWART and DEUCE MUSIC LIMITED
All Rights for ROD STEWART Controlled and Administered by EMI APRIL MUSIC INC.
All Rights Reserved   International Copyright Secured   Used by Permission

Our final batch of classic licks and phrases are by Stevie Ray Vaughan and run the gamut from relatively easy to exceedingly difficult in terms of overall technique and intricacy. The first is from "Pride and Joy" and uses open strings extensively. Stay in 1st position throughout the phrase so that your 2nd finger begins it with a G string bend and your 1st finger concludes it by trilling back and forth rapidly between the 1st fret and the open G string.

Open String Lick from "Pride and Joy" *(Stevie Ray Vaughan)*

The last four licks are from "Texas Flood," in the key of G. The slow tempo of this song allows for expansive and complex playing that packs each measure with blistering flurries of notes. The lick below stays in the 3rd position G minor pentatonic fingering for the first measure, with the 3rd finger reaching out to do the bending. Complete the bend, release, and pull-off in the second half of the measure by lifting off and pulling down enough to sound the G on the high E's 3rd fret as well as the D on the B string (your 1st finger should barre both strings). Begin measure 2 by shifting up to 6th position so that your 3rd finger performs the 8th fret bend and release. The last four notes bring us back down into 3rd position.

Bend and Shift Lick from "Texas Flood" *(Stevie Ray Vaughan)*

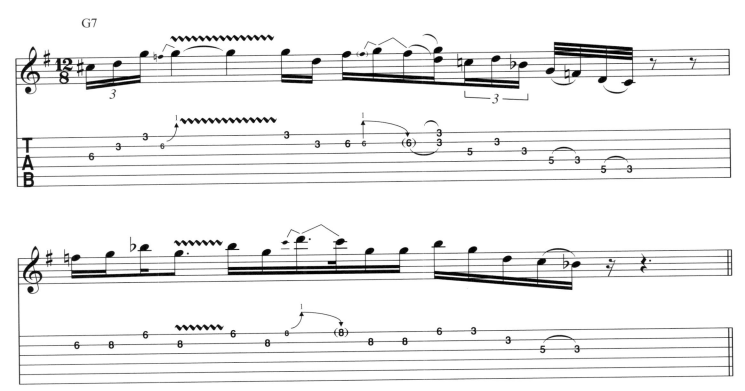

The next lick stays strictly in 3rd position, with the 3rd fingering doing all the bending save the final 1st finger bend on the G string. The notes are all taken from the G minor pentatonic scale with the addition of the major and ♭9ths (A and A♭ respectively), the ♭5th (D♭/C♯), and the major 3rd (B) played after the double bar. The rhythms are particularly tricky here, especially the first grouping: a septuplet stretched over one dotted quarter note beat in which the final note is replaced by a 32nd-note triplet! It's actually not quite as hard as it sounds; just make sure the entire grouping lasts one beat and you'll be pretty close. You may want to listen to the recording of this one to hear exactly how it should sound.

Pentatonic Lick with 9ths from "Texas Flood" *(Stevie Ray Vaughan)*

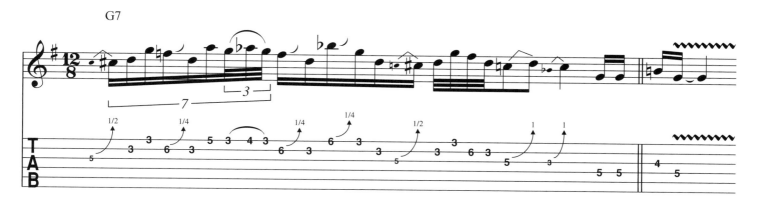

The following lick is played over the IV chord (C7) in measure 6 of the 12-bar form and finishes up as we move back to the I. Begin with a 3rd finger slide up the A string, then drop down to 3rd position on beat 4. Play each bend with your 3rd finger and grab the 6th fret F on the B string with your 4th finger. End by trilling back and forth between your 1st and 3rd fingers on the D string.

IV–I Lick from "Texas Flood" *(Stevie Ray Vaughan)*

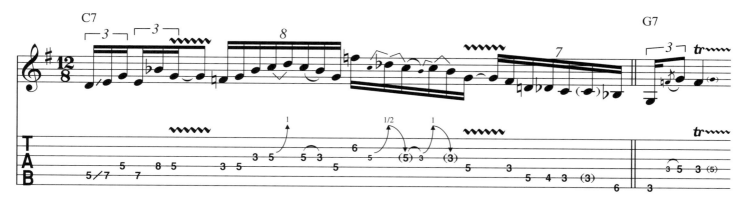

Our final lick is played over the V–IV (D7–C7) progression in measures 9 and 10 but works nearly as well in any other portion of the 12-bar form. The 3rd finger should perform each of the hammer-ons along the high E string at the start of the phrase, as well as each bend, save the final 1st finger bend on the G string. The pre-bends and releases in the second measure are particularly cool; just be sure you hit the targeted G note squarely on the nose each time to keep this one from sounding too sloppy.

V–IV Lick from "Texas Flood" *(Stevie Ray Vaughan)*

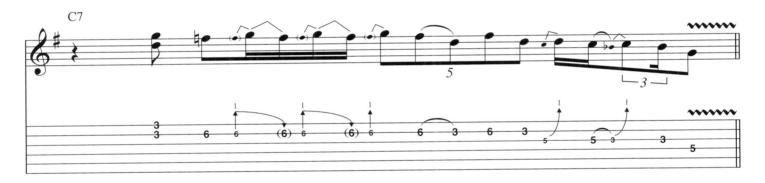

CHAPTER 8

Full Solos

Our final musical examples are the following five full-length solos, which include all of the techniques and classic vocabulary we've been studying to this point but also illustrate the larger goal of cohesive solo construction. Making the transition from stringing licks and phrases together to "hearing" your ideas and playing instinctively is a long process that requires one to simply do it over and over again. Ultimately, you want your imagination and ear to guide you and not just let your fingers do the walking and talking. Music begins in the mind, and the instrument is merely the tool for expressing what you conceive. We will elaborate on this point a bit in the closing chapter, but for now, let's take a look at these complete solo statements by the masters—beginning with B.B. King's solo from "Five Long Years."

At this point, the content below shouldn't be too challenging, technically speaking. The first five measures are played in 11th position, with the 3rd finger taking all the 13th fret bends. There are a handful of 1st finger bends on the 11th fret that require a bit more strength, as other fingers can't be enlisted to aid in the push. At the end of measure 5, drop down to 8th position quickly, then shift up to 13th position as measure 6 begins by sliding up the G string to the 14th fret with your 2nd finger. The final positional shift occurs in measure 11 when you drop back down to 8th position to finish out the solo. Take note of the careful use of rest and space throughout the solo. B.B. doesn't cram every measure full of notes or feel the need to prove his skill; he just plays with authority and relaxed, effortless mastery. The solo breathes, unfolds at a leisurely pace, and is always in the pocket rhythmically and totally grooving. While he does mix and match scales somewhat, blending major pentatonic tones with the predominant C minor pentatonic scale material, he generally keeps it simple and manipulates a few key notes and ideas throughout the solo, frequently returning to the most choice licks and milking them for all they're worth. This is confident, mature blues guitar with a powerful emotional punch.

Solo from "Five Long Years" *(B.B. King)*

TRACK 93, 0:00
Full Solo

TRACK 93, 0:53
Backing Track

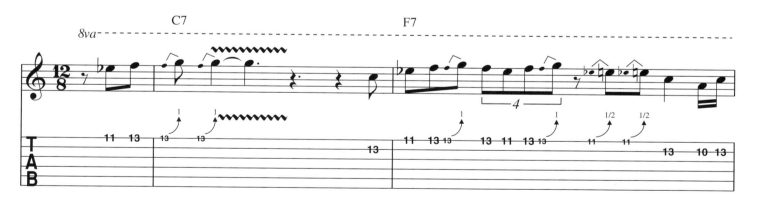

Next, let's check out Albert King's complete, two-chorus (24-bar) solo from "Crosscut Saw." Like B.B., Albert plays simply and powerfully, exploring a small set of crucial motifs, rather than throwing everything but the kitchen sink into his statements. The notes are taken exclusively from the A minor pentatonic scale, and King remains in the 5th position "box" fingering for the majority of the solo, leaving it only during the turnarounds at the end of each chorus and for some brief 3rd position sliding moves in a few select spots. The biggest technical hurdles here are the same ones encountered when tackling any Albert King work: the soaring overbends facilitated by hands of steel and a drop tuned guitar that lowers string tension considerably. You can try tuning down even further than the half step indicated here, but pushing that 8th fret, high E string C note all the way up to E will never be an easy task. Try not to snap the string as you practice this move! Once again, try to keep the big picture in mind: a solo shouldn't simply be a stringing together of licks, but should instead tell a story, with a beginning, middle, and end. It should be rhythmically accurate and organized, contrast density of notes with rests, and express an emotional state of mind or attitude—exuberant, sad, defiant, or whatever else you're feeling at the moment. Albert does all this and more.

Solo from "Crosscut Saw" *(Albert King)*

TRACK 94, 0:00
Full Solo

TRACK 94, 0:52
Backing Track

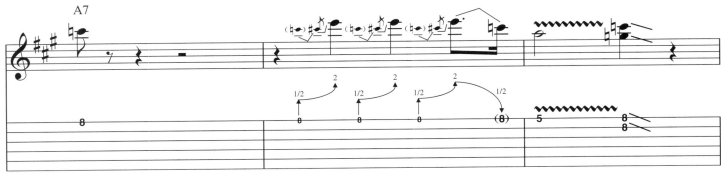

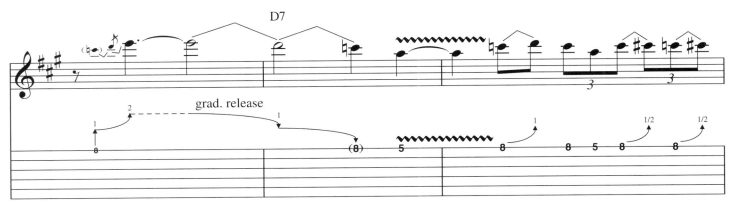

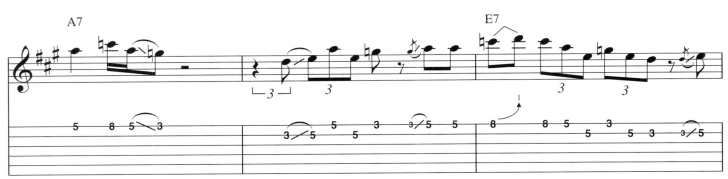

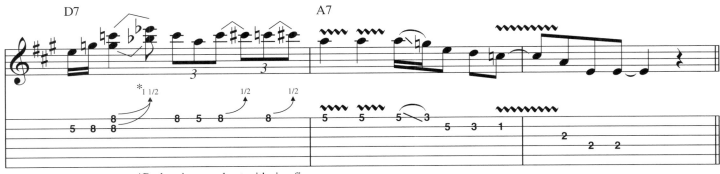

*Both strings are bent with ring finger.

Next up is the 12 bar "outro" solo that puts a cap on Stevie Ray Vaughan's "Pride and Joy." It's a great mix of single-note lines, double stops, and chords and really shows how much impact can be made in a single chorus. Contrast is big here, as register and rhythm vary greatly, and the single-note lines beginning in measure 6 really stand out and make the solo take off after the repeated double and triple stops in the earlier measures. Play these multi-note groupings with your 1st and 2nd fingers on the B and G strings, respectively, adding the open high E string to the mix as indicated. Measures 5 through 10 should be played in 12th position, with the 3rd finger doing all the 14th and 15th fret bending. The solo ends by dropping down into 1st position for some classic open string moves, followed by a rootless B9 chord and a final, sustained E7♯9 chord that gets a good shake with the tremolo bar.

Outro Solo from "Pride and Joy" *(Stevie Ray Vaughan)*

TRACK 95, 0:00
Full Solo

TRACK 95, 0:31
Backing Track

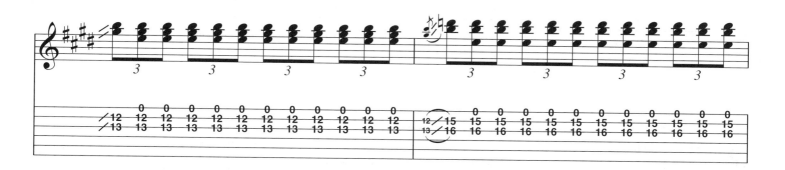

Written by Stevie Ray Vaughan
© 1985 RAY VAUGHAN MUSIC (ASCAP)/Administered by BUG MUSIC
All Rights Reserved   Used by Permission

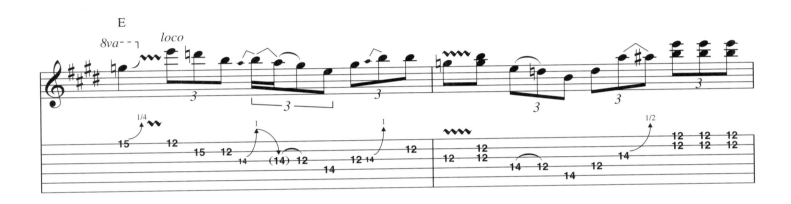

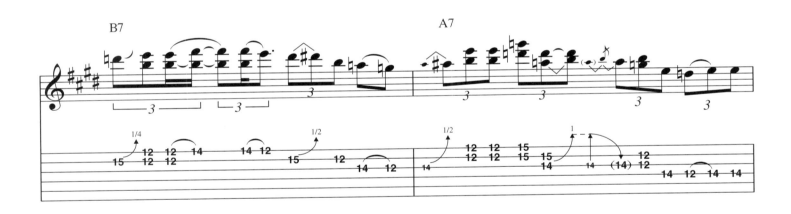

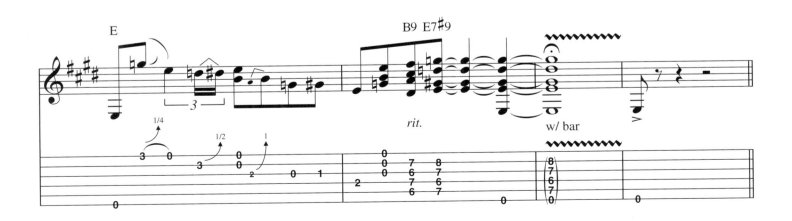

The excerpt below includes Eric Clapton's famous two-chorus solo from the beginning of "Hide Away," which is played in four distinct "regions" of the neck: 9th, 1st, 3rd, and 5th positions. Clapton in particular is fond of position shifting and often does a lot of lateral moving, illustrating the importance of knowing your scales and licks in a wide variety of keys, positions, and fingerings. The notes here are taken primarily from the E major pentatonic scale, with minor pentatonic additions used sparingly. The first seven measures stay strictly in 9th position, with the 3rd finger taking all the 11th fret bends, until the single-note lines are punctuated by sliding F7 and E7 chords. Drop down into 1st position at the end of measure 8 and play all 2nd fret notes with the 2nd finger. The trills in measures 11 and 23 should be played with the 1st finger hammering on and pulling off rapidly to the open G string. The slides up the same string to the 4th fret in measures 14 and 20 should be played by the 2nd finger, with the 1st finger grabbing the many D notes on the B string above. There's also a brief shift to 5th position in measures 18 and 19 beginning with an upwards rake that outlines an A major triad (A–C♯–E). All in all, it's a simple but memorable solo that explores just a handful of basic ideas, uses repetition effectively, and is always melodic and totally singable.

Intro Solo from "Hide Away" *(Eric Clapton)*

TRACK 96,
0:00
Full Solo

TRACK 96,
0:45
Backing Track

By Freddie King and Sonny Thompson
Copyright © 1961 by Fort Knox Music Inc. and Bug Music-Trio Music Company
Copyright Renewed
International Copyright Secured All Rights Reserved
Used by Permission

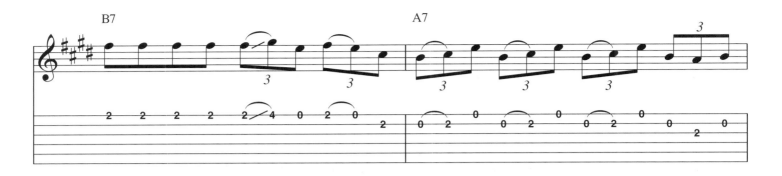

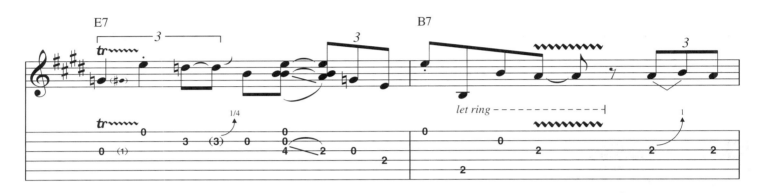

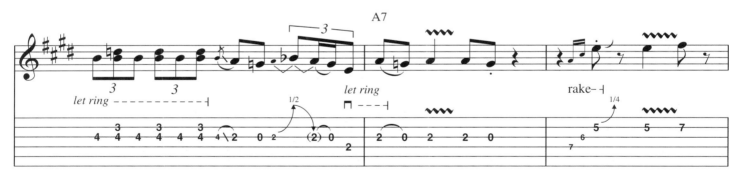

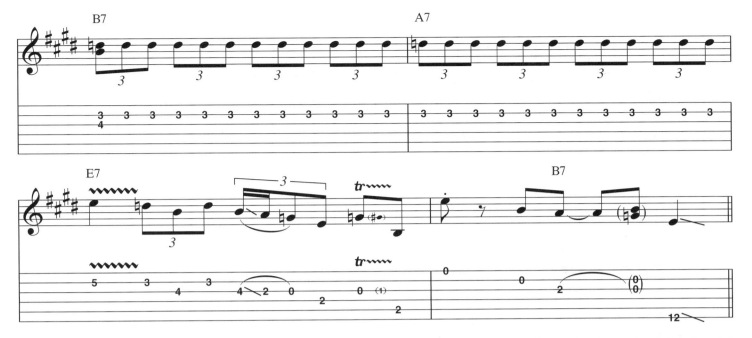

Finally, let's take a look at John Mayer's contemporary take on a classic and very traditional solo in the following 24 measure example in G. While the notes are taken primarily from the G minor pentatonic scale, there are quite a few additions along the way, including frequent use of the 9th (A), major 3rd (B), 6th (E), and ♭5th (D♭/C♯). The solo begins with a 2nd finger slide up the G string to the 9th fret, putting you in 8th position for the first six measures. After a percussive double stop in 6ths on the 15th and 16th frets, we drop down into 3rd position for two measures and then slide back up the neck to 15th position over the V chord (D7). This lick is then closely mirrored an octave lower in measure 10 and followed by a tasty turnaround laden with double stops. Mayer spends much of the second chorus in the 15th position G minor pentatonic "box," peppering his lines with 9ths and major 3rds (of both the C7 and G7 chords) in the process. The solo then concludes with a somewhat dissonant three-note chord (C♯–E–B♭) played over the G9 and D7 chords in both high and low registers and another beautifully crafted turnaround lick. Taken as a whole, it's a concise statement that reflects Mayer's intimate knowledge of the history and vocabulary of the style and his ability to craft melodic solos that are both authentic and highly personal. He's assimilated the work of his forebears and transformed it into something uniquely his own, while always remaining true to the spirit and essence of the blues.

Solo from "Come When I Call" *(John Mayer)*

TRACK 97, 0:00 — **Full Solo** **TRACK 97, 0:57** — **Backing Track**

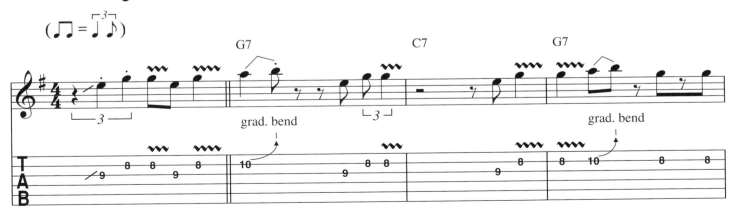

Words and Music by John Mayer

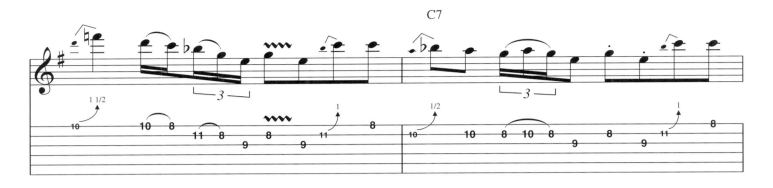

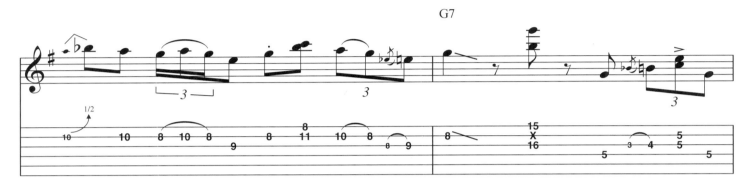

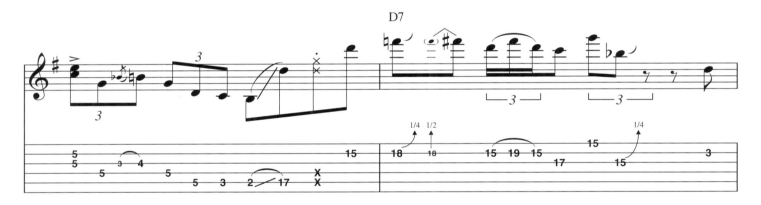

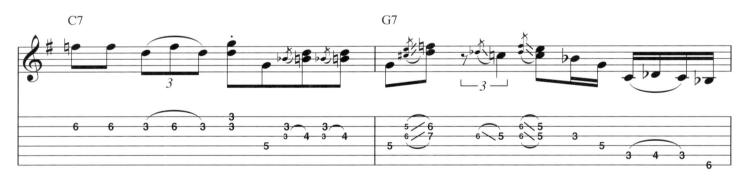

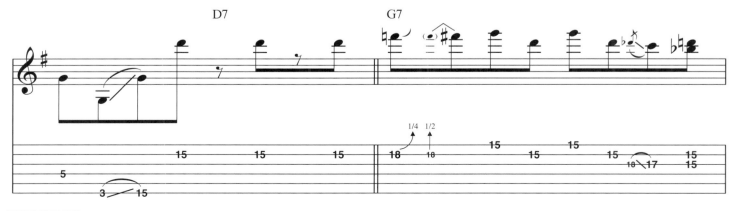

CHAPTER 9

Some Closing Thoughts

As we've worked our way through these pages, we've explored all of the essential technical components a blues guitar soloist will need. Take your time with the examples that illustrate them and learn to play your favorites in as many possible keys, positions, and registers as you can. This will go a long way towards their total assimilation into your playing and allow you to use them effectively and without contrivance. Let's wrap things up with a brief list of important concepts, reminders, and general tidbits of advice.

1. Play the solos you hear and not the ones your fingers lead you to. Some degree of scale-running, pattern-playing, and tossing out of licks is not only acceptable but expected; these things make up much of the shared vocabulary of the style. However, remind yourself that music begins in the imagination and not on the instrument, which is merely a tool for expressing yourself.

2. In keeping with the previous idea, get comfortable singing. That doesn't have to mean singing as if you're going on "American Idol" or even singing back-up on a local gig, but singing your ideas and things that you are learning from others as well. Sing in your car, sing in the shower, sing along with your favorite solos; it really doesn't matter. Try to sing your ideas and licks and don't worry if you're not totally in tune or sounding particularly pretty. The effect, once you have gotten used to this, is to help clarify your ideas and improve your phrasing and overall melodicism. It's also a great way to learn material, either from a book like this or from a recording. I often find that in teaching, when a student has trouble with a particular phrase or lick, putting down the guitar and singing the idea until it's clear will solve the problem, assuming it is within the reach of their given technical abilities and/or range, etc.. Often the problem isn't that one can't physically play it; it's that they don't actually know how it goes! Singing the phrase enough times will take care of this nicely.

3. Transcribe solos from recordings and write them down, or at the very least, memorize them and take your favorite phrases through the keys and positions of the neck. This is a fantastic way to learn the history and vocabulary of the blues and to improve your ear (and notational skills) to boot. The benefits of learning by ear are immense and should never be replaced simply by learning from books or other's transcriptions. Learn everything that appeals to you and go for a wide swath of players, eras, and sub-genres.

4. Never overlook rhythm as a vital force in improvisation. Albert King, Eric Clapton, and the rest of the greats all play pretty much the same notes as any fledgling blues guitarist or local guy sitting in at an open mic, so what separates them so clearly from the rest of us mere mortals? Aside from their very original musical conceptions, it's rhythm: the way a phrase unfolds, sits in the pocket, uses rest and space, or plays with or against the rhythm section. Singing helps solidify rhythmic ideas as much as melodic ones, and perhaps even more so, as it's hard to sing a million fast notes and bends but relatively easy to sing grooving, syncopated phrases and the like.

5. Play simply and within your abilities, without forcing anything technically or conceptually. Over time, your skill set will grow and consequently your ability to play this way will as well. Don't worry if you can't play as fast or as intricately as Stevie Ray Vaughan or Joe Bonamassa; practice will bring about the technical improvements you desire if you're diligent enough. Until then, stretch a bit, but generally stay contained and play what you hear and not what you think is going to impress.

6. Lastly, don't be a clone. Find your own voice. Many players spend their early careers in an emulation phase, and copying tons of Stevie Ray Vaughan stuff may be what you want to do right now…and you'll learn a lot that way. But eventually you have to make your own statement, because you can't be someone else; you'll never do their thing as well as they did or with their level of authenticity anyway. Play with emotion and honesty, expressing something, and try, without too much self-consciousness, to tell a story with your solos, giving them a beginning, middle (development), and end (climax). Take the listener somewhere with you and play a solo you'd want to sit down and listen to. Don't ramble on endlessly or use the rhythm section as a music-minus-one backing track. Play for yourself, play for the audience, and play for the other musicians. Have fun and never stop striving to improve. Make yourself into a better guitarist and communicator by playing as much as you can and putting in the time in the practice room. Good luck!